D0021147

Canon City Public Library
Canon City, Colorado

ALSO BY SUZE ORMAN

Suze Orman's 2009 Action Plan

Women & Money

The Money Book for the Young, Fabulous & Broke

The Laws of Money, the Lessons of Life

The Road to Wealth

The Courage to Be Rich

Suze Orman's Financial Guidebook

The 9 Steps to Financial Freedom

You've Earned It, Don't Lose It

Canon City Public Library
Canon City, Colorado

SUZE
ORMAN'S
ACTION PLAN

Revised and updated from
Suze Orman's 2009 Action Plan

SPIEGEL & GRAU

New York

2010

This book is designed to provide accurate and authoritative information about personal finances. Neither the author nor the
publisher is engaged in rendering legal accounting, or other professional services, by publishing this book. If any such assistance
is required, the services of a qualified financial professional should
be sought. The author and publisher will not be responsible for any
liability, loss, or risk incurred as a result of the use and application
of any of the information contained in this book.

While the author has made every effort to provide accurate tele-
phone numbers and Internet addresses at the time of publication,
neither the publisher nor the author assumes any responsibility
for errors or for changes that occur after publication.

A Certified Financial Planner® is a federally registered mark
owned by the Certified Financial Planner Board of Standards, Inc.

2010 Spiegel & Grau Mass Market Edition

Copyright © 2008, 2010 by Suze Orman, a Trustee of the
Suze Orman Revocable Trust

All rights reserved.

Published in the United States by Spiegel & Grau, an imprint
of The Random House Publishing Group, a division of
Random House, Inc., New York.

SPIEGEL & GRAU and Design is a registered trademark of
Random House, Inc.

Originally published in paperback and in different form
in the United States by Spiegel & Grau, an imprint of
The Random House Publishing Group, a division
of Random House, Inc., in 2008.

ISBN 978-0-8129-8155-1

Printed in the United States of America

www.spiegelandgrau.com

2 4 6 8 9 7 5 3 1

CONTENTS

SUZE
ORMAN'S
ACTION PLAN

1
All Eyes on the Road Ahead

Exhale. The eye of the financial hurricane has passed. The storm that hit in the summer of 2008 and continued to batter the global economy and your personal finances through 2009 is slowly—ever so slowly—receding. The worst is over. You survived. We survived.

Now comes the really hard work: rebuilding.

IRAs, 401(k)s and 529 college savings plans must be rebuilt in the wake of the devastating bear market.

Budgets have to be put in place that account for the new world order in which the penalties for having credit card debt and no emergency savings are unthinkable. You know as well as I do: You must find a way to get rid of the debt and build your savings.

Your approach to homeownership must be rebuilt to reflect this simple truth: A home is not a liquid investment that will always rise in value. It is shelter, first and foremost. It can also be a terrific asset, but only if you approach it with clear-eyed expectations.

Most important, your sense of security must be rebuilt. There's the not so small issue of our collective national bill for what has happened; the current $1.4 trillion federal deficit is expected to rise to $9 trillion by 2019. But on a more personal note you are grappling with the realization that your pre-crash way of life is over. What worked—or more correctly, what you thought worked—is gone, leaving you without your bearings in these new times.

Now that we have weathered the worst of the storm, you're onto the next challenge: Where do we go from here?

Toward Lasting Security

When I wrote the original *Action Plan* for 2009, it was with a laser focus on getting you through the crisis as it was unfolding. My goal was to give you the tools to find your footing in a world where the ground was shifting—and shifting violently—beneath you. As the year progressed and I heard from so many of you—in person, via Twitter, and through my CNBC show—I realized that you were hungry for more than crisis-management strategies. You have moved on to future management. You want to know the right actions to take in order to build lasting security.

You have been shaken to your core. Whether it is because of fear, regret, or remorse, living through the tumult of the financial meltdown has given you newfound purpose. You want to be in control, you want to get it right. No more fly-by-the-seat-of-your-pants, enjoy-the-ride-while-it-lasts mentality. No more trusting that things will work out, that someone else—your financial advisor, the regulators in Washington—have your back. You understand what is at stake. You are personally accountable and responsible for building and sustaining financial security. You just need a new game plan to transform your resolve into reality.

New Rules for New Times

Because so much has changed in the world and in your worldview, I decided to publish a new *Action Plan*. I think of it as *Action Plan* v. 2.0: The Long-Term View. I have updated the information and advice to take into account changes that have occurred since the fall of 2008, such as new pro-consumer credit card legislation and the Treasury Department's broad Making Home Affordable initiative designed to keep more Americans from losing their homes. Each chapter now begins with a fresh introduction focused on "New Rules for

New Times." During the heat of the crisis my advice was to show you how to keep your money safe and secure. That's still in play, of course, but now it's time to move forward with strategies that will build security for you this year, next year, and beyond. That requires an understanding of what works now—and what doesn't—in every aspect of your financial life, from credit management to retirement planning to saving for a child's college education.

Three universal rules govern all the specific advice in the following chapters:

Rule #1: Let go of the past. There is no way you can move forward if you are still holding on to what "used to be." As in: "My 401(k) used to be worth . . ." or "My house used to be valued at . . ." or "My job used to be secure" or "My credit card rate used to be 5%." You can't get where you want to go—where you need to go—if you are looking in the rearview mirror. All eyes on the road ahead. All decisions must be based on what is real today, not what used to be.

Rule #2: Plan on moderation. As I write this in the fall of 2009, the tea leaves suggest that the official recession is over and the recovery is beginning to gain momentum. But it will be a recovery of moderation, a state of affairs that has been dubbed "the new normal." Instead of growing at the 3% annual clip that persisted for the past few decades, Gross Domestic Product (GDP) is expected to rise at a more moderate 2% rate in the new normal. That slower growth will ripple throughout the economy and your finances. Stock returns are expected to be more moderate, as are the prospects for home values. And without a booming economy, higher unemployment could be a fixture of the new normal; businesses are expected to take a slow-go approach to increasing their payroll as they grapple with the ramifications of more moderate growth and profits. New times indeed.

I also want you to understand that while the worst is over, we are not completely out of the woods. To repeat what I said a year ago: I expect we will be on a roller coaster until 2014 or 2015, because the markets, the economy, and the entire global financial system will need time to fully digest the toxic assets that still abound on many balance sheets.

Rule #3: Respect risk. Absent from the conversation throughout the stock and real estate bubbles was this crucial calculation: "What is the risk?" It's as if everyone refused to entertain the possibility that risk existed. During the Internet stock bubble, you bought into the argument that we were at the dawn of paradigm shift—remember how often we heard that one?—that would see market gains more than double the historical rate and sustain them. When the 2000–2003 bear market hit, you were shocked—*shocked!*—to see your stock portfolio get creamed. And it never occurred to you, during the real estate bubble, that home values would ever—*could* ever—fall. It wasn't just you; the trends and data Wall Street used to fuel much of the real estate mania didn't even address the possibility that home values could decline! And let's just say that Washington regulators also seemed to be asleep at the wheel in terms of managing systemic risk.

So much of the carnage could have been avoided if every one of us—individuals and institutions—had respected risk. Notice I said respect, not avoid. The goal is to stop at every juncture and make sure you understand the potential risk, and then make a conscious and deliberate decision on how to mitigate that risk. Owning a home is very risky when done with an exotic mortgage whose initial rate is artificially low but can skyrocket when it resets. Owning a home with a fixed-rate mortgage in which the monthly amount due is the same in month one as in month 360 (30 years down the line) is a whole lot less risky. An IRA invested 100% in stocks when you are in your 50s or 60s is very risky. An IRA that holds bonds and cash is a whole lot less risky.

The call to action is that you must be your own risk manager. Yes, we all should expect Washington regulators to do a better job, and let's hope they will. But you can't afford to rely on this; you must assess your own tolerance for risk and understand the stakes. Your own resolve and vigilance will keep you from being hoodwinked by the next bubble. That's right—I said the next bubble. Bubbles have long been a part of our history, for better or worse. That doesn't mean they have to threaten your financial life; it is up to you whether you buy into them or choose to watch from the sidelines.

It's All Good News

Feeling down? Feeling like this is so depressing? Okay, enough of that. Listen to me: This is a phenomenal opportunity. When you are so shaken you know you will do everything never to revisit that feeling, you have all the motivation you need to get it right once and for all. A year ago I wrote the *Action Plan* to help you survive the crisis. Now my focus is to give you the tools to thrive. Yes, *thrive*. That's what you deserve, is it not? Not just this year, but every year.

The tragedy of the financial crisis is that it has robbed so many of you of what is most important: living your life to the fullest. You are stuck obsessing about money. You are worried sick about money. But the truth is, worry doesn't fix a thing. Action does. So let's get started.

2

ACTION PLAN

Credit

New Rules for New Times

This is one breakup that makes me really happy. I know it is painful for you, but trust me, the cold shoulder you are getting from the credit card industry is the best thing that could have happened to you.

I'm just sorry this unhealthy relationship dragged on for so long. For years you, the American Consumer, were on an insatiable spending spree. Unstoppable spending seemed to be downright patriotic. So what if you lacked the income to pay for all those purchases? Why worry about that small detail when you could just ring up a tab on your credit cards?

Credit card issuers were willing suitors. They plied you with near-daily offers of new credit; in 2007 consumers were flooded with an estimated

5.2 billion credit card offers, or about 23 for each American over the age of 18. The offers often came with 0% teaser rates and balance-transfer terms that encouraged you to keep up the charade of believing you have more money than you do. By the end of 2007 the nation had collective credit debt of more than $950 billion. (Yes, *billion*.) Yet it was far from free money. The banks collected an estimated $18 billion in late-payment fees and billions more in interest charges. The credit card industry saw their profits rise $27 billion over 2003 levels. Wow.

Then suddenly it was all over. As the credit crisis gained velocity, beginning in the summer of 2008, many banks had a chilling change of heart. They cut credit lines, closed down accounts, and raised fees and interest rates in an effort to protect their balance sheets from rising payment delinquencies. That continued throughout 2009, as the highest unemployment rate in 26 years sent the delinquency rate even higher.

So here we are: Many of you are nursing a painful case of withdrawal that includes everything from pangs of regret to moments of anger for being dumped so unceremoniously. After years of spending with impunity, you not only couldn't borrow more, you now face huge financial penalties on your existing balances. Even people with sparkling credit scores and pristine credit reports were caught in the maelstrom; a FICO credit score of 800 provided no protection from a credit line cut.

The about-face turned by so many banks couldn't have come at a worse time for those of you using your credit lines as virtual emergency savings funds. Your plan was that if you ever needed to cover an unexpected expense, you'd just charge it or take a cash advance. But just when layoffs, furloughs, and pay cuts hit with a vengeance during the recession, your financial lifeline vanished.

As wrenching as the credit squeeze has been, I have to tell you that it presents a wonderful opportunity to catapult you to a happier and more secure way of life. You've no doubt heard the saying "Once bitten, twice shy." After what you have been through, or watched friends and family cope with, my hope is that you are now sufficiently motivated to never allow yourself to be bitten again. Please do not let yourself fall victim to your own faulty assumptions and poor spending choices or to the fickle and costly practices of the credit card industry.

For make no mistake: The days of easy credit will return. Maybe not as easy as it was in years past, but certainly not as tight as 2008–2009. It's the nature of the credit industry to give credit. Make it your business once and for all to be smart and powerful in how you choose to use credit.

The New Rules for Credit mean you pay as you go. The closer you can get to being able to pay off your credit card balances at the end of each month—

that is, not owing the card issuer a dime in interest—the closer you are to financial freedom.

Your first job is to clean up any existing mess that may exist. If you don't already have an emergency savings fund in place, dealing with your credit card debt has to move to second place on your to-do list. My recommendation is that you first use your available cash to build up a solid federally insured savings account at a bank or credit union. You can't rely on your credit card to be a backup emergency fund. It was never ideal, and as I explain later in this chapter, it became an extremely dangerous gambit in 2009.

Once you have the savings account in place, you are ready to tackle your credit card debt. It may take you three months or three years to work your way out of the hole. Just vow to stay focused on the endgame: no longer being at the mercy of the credit card industry.

What you must do

- If you have an eight-month emergency savings fund, make it a priority to pay off your credit card balances.
- If you do not have an eight-month emergency savings fund and you have credit card debt, look into a balance transfer to a credit union credit card. Then split your money between building up your emergency savings and paying down your credit card debt.

- If you have a high-rate credit card and you cannot transfer to a lower-rate card, and you do not have an eight-month emergency fund, pay just the minimum on your card and focus on increasing your emergency savings.
- Read every statement and all correspondence from your credit card company to make sure you are aware of any changes to your account, such as skyrocketing interest rates.
- Work to get your FICO credit score above 740.
- Be very careful where you turn to for help with credit card debt. Debt consolidators are often a very bad deal. The National Foundation for Credit Counseling is a smarter choice.
- Resist the temptation to use retirement savings or a home equity line of credit to pay off credit card debt.
- Vow to use your credit responsibly.

Your Action Plan: Credit

SITUATION: You always pay the minimum amount due on your credit card bill and are never late, but your credit card limit was just reduced.

ACTION: Just paying the minimum sends a huge warning signal to your credit card company. It's a tip-off that you may already be on shaky ground. To be sure, in flush times, credit card companies didn't worry about this too much, but when the going gets tough, credit card companies get scared that you will be unable to repay your debt. As we saw throughout 2009, credit card companies aggressively cut the credit limits or closed down the accounts of customers they deemed the most risky.

If you have an eight-month emergency savings account tucked away, then paying more than the minimum due on your credit card bills is a smart way to try and avoid a credit-limit cut. But if you do not have that emergency savings fund in place, I am not recommending that you push yourself to make higher payments on your credit card debt. You must make it your first priority to build up a savings account. If that means you continue to make only the minimum payments due so you have money to put toward your emergency savings fund, that is the trade-off you may need to make. It is not ideal, but it is realistic. It is a temporary necessity—a provisional game plan until your safety net is securely in place. Yes, paying the minimum amount due may lead to having your credit limit cut. But in 2009 even customers who made bigger payments to get their balances paid down saw their credit limits cut and their accounts closed. That created a bigger problem. If you had used all your cash to pay off the debt and then still had the card limit cut (or the account closed), how were you to cover emergencies? You had no lifelines left.

The reality is that you cannot rely on your credit

card to work as an ad-hoc emergency savings fund. As so many of you learned in 2009, just when you need to use your credit line you may find it sharply reduced or even revoked. So that's why I say you need to make the best of a bad situation: There can be negative repercussions to continuing to pay just the minimum due on your credit card, but it is still the smarter move so you will have more money available to build up an emergency savings account. (Later in this chapter I explain a strategy that, if feasible for you, can enable you to simultaneously build savings and pay down your card debt.)

SITUATION: You have a sparkling credit score, have always paid your entire balance due at the end of each month, yet your credit limit was cut.

ACTION: In the wake of the financial crisis, credit card companies were looking everywhere to reduce their risk. Even customers with FICO credit scores of 800 or better (any score between 720 and 850 is considered the gold standard) saw their credit limits reduced. This had nothing to do with the customer; it was all about credit card companies wanting to reduce the outstanding limits they had on their own balance sheets.

If your monthly credit card bills amount to less than 10% to 20% of your remaining credit limits (on all your cards), you need not worry. Your FICO credit score will not be hurt. The only potential problem is if a credit-limit cut causes your debt-to-credit limit (explained in full later in this section) to rise above 25%. That can indeed cause a big hit—50 points or more—to a high FICO score. You might consider opening one new account to add more available credit and help keep your overall debt-to-credit ratio low. Opening a new credit card might cause a slight dip in your credit score over the short term, but it buys you long-term insurance to protect yourself from a bigger score reduction if your credit limit is cut and sends your debt-to-credit ratio soaring. And I know I can trust you to use that card responsibly, right? After all, you just told me you have a sparkling FICO score.

SITUATION: You always pay the minimum due each month, but your card company just changed how they calculate the minimum, and now you owe a lot more each month.

ACTION: I realize this is a bitter pill if you are already financially stressed, but being forced to pay a higher minimum is actually good medicine for your long-term financial health. The more you send in each month, the faster your balance will be paid off. Now, that said, the timing of this change is ridiculous. It makes me so angry that the same people who seduced consumers into

super-low minimum payments during the good
times (the lower your payment, the more the card
company earned in interest on the unpaid balance)
are now applying the screws when so many families are already stretched so thin. Some card issuers have raised the minimum due each month from
2% of the balance to 5%.

If you can afford the higher payments, grit your
teeth and pay them. As I said, the more you pay
now, the better. If that's not feasible, read my advice later in this chapter on transferring your
balance to a credit union credit card. Credit unions
typically charge much lower interest rates on
credit card balances. And be sure to check
out my advice in "Action Plan: Spending" on ways
to find more money in your budget to put toward
financial goals, such as paying off your credit
card balance. If you absolutely know you can't afford the higher payment, call up the credit card
issuer and see if you can negotiate a workout.
The card company may be willing to convert
your credit card balance to a fixed-interest-rate
loan that you repay over a set period of, say, two to
five years. But there's a trade-off: The card will
be canceled, and that can end up hurting your
FICO score. But that's a price you may need to
pay to deal with this situation. The bottom line is
that the sooner you get out from under the credit
card company's claws, the better off you will be
financially.

SITUATION: You had a backup emergency card tucked in your desk that you never used, and now the credit card company just told you it is reducing the credit limit.

ACTION: Once again, I need to be clear here: Credit card companies can cut limits any time they want and for any reason. And to be honest, if they see you aren't using your card, that's an easy call for them. But as I explained above, when credit limits are cut it can have a negative impact on your FICO credit score. If you have already been hit with a credit limit cut, consider opening one new card so you have a new credit limit to add to your account. Obviously, I want you to do this only if you are a stellar manager of credit cards; this advice is for those of you who have FICO scores of 720 plus and aren't a risk to mismanage new credit. Once you get the new card, use it at least once a month to keep it active.

If you are someone who has an emergency card tucked away unused, I want you to dust it off and put it to use every month. An active card can be less likely to be hit with a credit-limit reduction. This is not an excuse to spend more. I simply want you to shift one of your existing expenses to this card. You don't even need to carry it in your wallet; move one of your recurring monthly payments onto this card and you're set. Just remember to pay the bill on time.

SITUATION: You are worried that a lower credit limit will hurt your FICO credit score.

ACTION: Pay off your balance every month and your FICO credit score will not be affected. Your FICO credit score is based on a series of calculations that measure how good a credit risk you are. One of the biggest factors in your credit score—accounting for about 30% of your score—is how much debt you have. There are a few ways that this specific calculation is done, but one of the chief ways it's determined is the debt-to-available-credit ratio. Debt is how much money you owe on all your credit cards. Available credit is the sum of all the credit lines that have been extended to you. The higher your debt, the worse it is for your FICO score. And your debt-to-credit ratio will look much worse if your credit limit is cut.

Let's say you have only one credit card that has a $2,000 balance on it. Last year your credit limit on that card was $10,000. So your debt-to-credit ratio was 20% ($2,000 is 20% of $10,000). Now you find out that your credit card company has reduced your credit line to $5,000. That means your ratio shoots up to 40% ($2,000 is 40% of $5,000). That will indeed have a negative impact on your FICO score.

The only way to keep your FICO score unaffected by a credit-limit reduction is to get out of credit card debt and pay off your bills in full each month. But if you don't yet have an eight-month emergency savings fund, you need to be strategic on what task to focus on. Later in this chapter I explain how to handle credit card debt if you have yet to build an eight-month emergency savings fund.

SITUATION: You pay your credit card bill in full each month, so you're surprised your FICO score isn't better. When you investigated, you were told that your score would be better if your debt-to-credit ratio was lower.

ACTION: Even if you pay your bill in full each month, you likely will have a debt-to-credit ratio that is above zero. You need to understand that your credit score is calculated by taking a quick snapshot of your finances right when the score request is made—by you, or by a lender. If the request comes a week before you have paid your credit card bill, it may show the current unpaid balance. For example, let's say you have a $10,000 credit limit and this month you have $3,000 in new charges that you intend to pay in full well before the bill is due. If your score "snapshot" is taken before you have paid the bill—even if you pay on time—your debt-to-credit limit will nonetheless show up as 30%, and that can affect your FICO score. One way around this is to boost your total credit limit by getting a new card, but only if you promise you will not increase your spending (just shift some charges to your new card).

I also advise anyone who is about to apply for a mortgage or a car loan to try to limit their credit card purchases. Not using the credit card at all for two months before you apply for a loan is ideal; that's the only way to ensure that when your credit score is "pulled" by a lender your debt-to-credit ratio will be zero.

SITUATION: The credit card company canceled your account. Do you still have to pay the remaining balance?

ACTION: Of course you do! When your account is canceled, it is because the credit card company has labeled you a high-risk cardholder. What is being canceled is your ability to use that card in the future. But you are still responsible for every penny of your existing balance.

SITUATION: Your credit card has been canceled and you are worried it will hurt your FICO score.

ACTION: Focus on getting the balance paid off; the lower the balance, the less it will damage your FICO score if your card is canceled.

There are two issues that come up when a card is canceled: how it affects your debt-to-credit-limit ratio and what happens to the interest rate on your unpaid balance. In many cases, when a card that has a balance on it has been revoked or canceled, the credit card company will immediately raise your interest rate to about 30%. When this happens, if you continue to pay only the minimum monthly payment, you may never get out of debt on that card.

SITUATION: You thought the interest rate on your credit card was fixed at 5%, but it just shot up to 30%!

ACTION: There is no such thing as a permanent fixed interest rate on your credit card. The rate is fixed only until the credit card issuer decides it isn't. It's a marketing ploy. And credit card companies have all sorts of reasons (embedded in the agreement you accepted when you opened the card) to raise your rate.

But Congress pushed through changes—finally!—that regulate how card companies can manipulate your rates. Beginning in February 2010, as long as you make timely payments on an existing balance—even just the minimum—your interest rate cannot be increased on that balance. If you fall more than 60 days behind on your payments, the card company has the right to raise your interest rate. But if you then get back on track and make six months of on-time payments, your rate must then revert to the lower rate. That is, six months of good behavior means the penalty rate expires.

Another new regulation beginning in February 2010 stipulates that as long as you are on time with your payments, the credit card company can raise your interest rate on only new charges, and even then it must give you 45 days' advance notice of its new policy.

If you want to steer clear of being hit with a giant rate hike, don't run up a balance in the first place. Or if you do have an unpaid balance, make sure you make timely minimum payments at the very least. Beginning in February 2010, you will find some measure of protection from any future hikes on that existing balance if you can observe these rules. But let me be clear, the absolute best action is to get your balance paid off in full, pronto. When you have a zero balance, what do you care about the interest rate?

SITUATION: You have a low-interest-rate credit card you never use—it is just there in case of emergency. Now you're worried that if you have to use it, your interest rate will go up.

ACTION: Build a real emergency savings account. Relying on your credit card to bail you out of emergencies is too dangerous. (See "Action Plan: Saving" for advice on where to open a savings account and "Action Plan: Spending" for action steps on how to come up with more money to put toward a savings fund.)

If you use a credit card for an emergency expense and you can't pay off the balance, you will set off a vicious cycle. An unpaid balance where there once was none makes a credit card company nervous. It can also make other credit card companies you have accounts with nervous. That could cause the credit limits on all your cards to be cut. And if that causes your FICO credit score to drop, then you can expect the interest rate on your credit card to rise.

The only solution is to stop thinking of your credit card as a safety net if you run into trouble. The only true safety net is a savings account.

SITUATION: You have a FICO credit score above 720 but your interest rate just shot up. What's the best way to pay off your credit card debt?

ACTION: See if you can apply for a balance transfer to a low-rate card. Because you have a high FICO score, you may be in luck. I recommend checking out credit cards offered through credit unions. By law credit unions are currently allowed to charge a maximum 18% APR on credit card balances. That's a lot better than the 30% or more many bank credit card issuers are charging these days! And with a strong FICO score you have a good shot at qualifying for a single-digit interest rate on a credit union card. Go to creditcardconnection.org for the best deals on credit union cards.

The idea is to move your money to a card with a

low introductory rate and then push yourself to get the balance paid off before the low rate expires. Please read the fine print very carefully. For example, the great rate typically applies only to the balances that are transferred; new charges you make on the card often will carry a higher interest rate. There's also the added problem that many balance transfer deals now charge a flat 3% fee on the entire amount transferred. That can quickly add up. My best advice is to push yourself to pay off the balance, rather than rely on a transfer. Even a low interest rate on a credit union card still costs you plenty. The best action—now and forever—is to get out of debt, period. But if you need an interim plan while you are turning over your new spending leaf, then definitely look into a credit union credit card. Then push yourself to get that balance polished off. In "Action Plan: Spending," I explain how to reassess your family's income and expenses to find more money to put toward paying down credit card debt.

SITUATION: You have a low FICO credit score, but you are current on all your accounts. How should you deal with your debt?

ACTION: Here's how:

■ Pay the minimum amount due on every card each month. That's your only shot at keeping your FICO score from falling further. It will also lower the odds that your credit card company will close your account, though a low FICO score may be enough to trigger a cut or cancellation.

- If you have at least a five-month emergency savings account and you can move your balance to a credit union card with an interest rate below 10%, divide your monthly savings between building up your emergency fund (eight months is still the goal) and paying off more of your credit card balance. For example, let's say that the minimum due on your credit card this month is $100 and you have $300 to put toward your financial goals. That leaves you with $200 above what must go to the minimum payment. I want you to split that $200 in half: $100 goes into the emergency fund and $100 is added to your credit card payment (meaning you will pay a total of $200 to the credit card this month). There is no substitute for having real savings set aside so you can handle life's inevitable surprises and emergencies.

- If you don't have an eight-month emergency savings fund and you can't transfer your high-rate balance to a lower-rate credit union card: I want you to pay just the minimum due on your credit card and keep building your emergency fund. If you are stuck with a bank card that charges you 20% or 30% and you face the very real risk that even if you pay off the card you will see your card shut down or your credit limit cut, you need to build your own savings—and fast. I want to repeat that this is not an ideal situation, but it is just too risky for you to be without an emergency savings fund.

- If you cannot transfer all your credit card debt to one card—preferably a low-rate credit union card, here's how to tackle balances on multiple cards: Line up your cards and put the card that charges the highest interest rate at the top of the pile. That's the card you focus on paying off first. Send in as much money as you can each month to get that balance down to zero.

- Once the first card is paid off, focus on the second card in your pile: the card with the next-highest interest rate.

- Keep up with this system until you have all the cards paid off.

Of course, the big challenge is finding extra money every month to put toward paying off your credit card debt. In "Action Plan: Spending," I have suggestions about how to "find" more money in your month by reducing your expenses.

SITUATION: You are behind on your credit card payments, but you want to know the best payment strategy for improving your FICO score.

ACTION: Focus on paying the most you can on accounts that are the least late. The longer unpaid debt has been on your credit reports, the less effect it has on your FICO score. So if you can make current an account that is past due by only 60 days, it will help your FICO score far more than paying off your balance on an account you have been past due on for three years. I want you to organize your credit card statements into two piles: cards that are past due for less than one year and those that are past due for more than one year. Start with the first pile: Pay off the account that is closest to being current first, then move to the next card in that pile. Once you have paid off the cards in the first pile, I want you to use the strategy I covered in the action step above for paying off cards that you are more than one year behind on.

SITUATION: You want to use your HELOC to pay off your credit card debt.

ACTION: Do not do this. Even if you still have enough equity to keep your HELOC open, this is a dangerous mistake. You are putting your house at risk. When you borrow from your HELOC, your home is the collateral. Let's say you get laid off or face a furlough—as we all saw, and many experienced, in 2009, that's a fact of life during recessions—and suddenly you can't keep up with the HELOC payments on top of all your other bills. Fall behind on the payments and you could lose your house.

As much as I want you to pay off your credit card debt, you need to understand that credit card debt is "unsecured" debt. There is no collateral that a credit card company can easily force you to hand over to settle your debt. So it makes no sense to transfer your unsecured debt into a secured debt—a HELOC—where you run the risk of losing your home if you can't make the payments.

SITUATION: You want to take out a loan from your 401(k) to pay off your credit card debt.

ACTION: Do not do this. I know it is tempting, but it is such a dangerous move. Anyone who has been listening to my advice over the years knows I have never approved of 401(k) loans because you end up paying tax twice on the money you borrow. But I can understand that if you are staring at an interest rate of 30% on your credit card, you figure the tax penalty is worth paying.

Again, I need you to focus on the possibility of losing your job. I don't care how valued an employee you are, in rough times we are all vulnerable. And even in good times, you can't tell me there is a guarantee your company won't ever choose to downsize, revamp, or send some jobs to less expensive markets, domestic or foreign. Look, I hope you never have to deal with any of those scenarios, but my job is to make sure you are prepared to handle the possibility that you may face a job loss at some point. *Any* point.

If you have an outstanding loan against your 401(k) when you are laid off, you typically must pay off the loan within a short period of time. Fail to do that and it becomes a withdrawal; that means you owe tax on the entire amount immediately and a 10% early-withdrawal penalty if you are under age 55 in the year you left service. And tell me exactly where you will get the money for that. Not your credit card, that's for sure.

An even bigger issue is that you need your 401(k) for tomorrow. Use it today and what will you have in retirement? Can't think about that right now? Excuse me, you can't afford *not* to think about that. And that brings me to the issue of bankruptcy. I certainly hope this never happens to you, but in the event you must declare bankruptcy, one silver lining is that any money you have in a 401(k) or IRA is protected. That is, you will not be required to use your retirement savings to settle your debts. It is a permanent asset for you. Don't blow it by using the money to pay off your credit card debt.

SITUATION: You have heard that credit card companies may be willing to reach a settlement for a reduced payment. Who's a likely candidate?

ACTION: You must be seriously behind in your payments and have a sizable lump sum of cash at the ready to have any shot at working out a settlement that reduces what you owe.

The only way the credit card company will forgive a portion of your unpaid balance is if you can make a lump-sum payment that covers some of the money you owe. Let's say you have $20,000 in credit card debt that the credit card company is willing to reduce to $10,000. You need to be able to pay cold cash to cover the remaining $10,000 immediately. This is not about getting your balance lowered and then promising to be a good Boy Scout or Girl Scout who will stick to a monthly repayment plan. To get a settlement requires having enough cash at the ready to pay off the entire remaining (reduced) balance. If you don't have that money, you aren't likely to be offered a settlement deal.

SITUATION: You wonder if negotiating a settlement will hurt your FICO credit score.

ACTION: If you don't want your FICO score to go down, do not ask for a settlement. A settlement means you failed to live up to your obligation to pay the full amount of debt you were responsible for. It will indeed have a negative impact on your credit score. That said, in certain rare instances—if you've previously had a stellar record, have suffered a job loss or medical catastrophe, and the outstanding debt isn't huge—you may be able to convince the card issuer not to report the settlement. Be prepared to document your case.

SITUATION: You just received a tax document from the credit card company that says it reported the amount of your settlement to the IRS.

ACTION: Be prepared to pay income tax on the amount of the forgiven credit card debt.

By law, the credit card company is required to send you and the IRS a 1099-C form that shows the amount of the forgiven debt, which is indeed money that you will owe income tax on. Sorry, there is no tax break for credit card settlements. (An exception is if you are insolvent, meaning the amount of all your liabilities is more than the value of all your assets. If the forgiven debt is reported to the IRS on a Form 1099, you should attach a note to your tax return explaining the insolvency—otherwise, the IRS will likely initiate an automatic audit, since the income reported on the 1099 does not appear on your return. Be prepared with good documentation to back up your claim that at the time the debt was forgiven, your liabilities exceeded the fair market value of your assets. I recommend you work with a tax advisor to help you navigate this situation.)

SITUATION: You hold a credit card from a bank that failed. What's going to happen to your account?

ACTION: The best protection is a strong FICO score. When one bank fails, another bank takes on its existing credit card accounts. But you need to realize that the new bank is not required to keep offering you that card. It will investigate your account and decide if you are a good credit risk. And let's be honest here: If your bank failed in part because it was too lenient about extending credit, it stands to reason that the acquiring bank may not want to keep your business. Bottom line: If you are a credit risk, your credit card could be shut down. If you have a strong FICO score, you will no doubt be welcomed by the new bank with open arms.

SITUATION: You hold a credit card from a bank that failed. Do you still need to pay off your balance?

ACTION: Of course you are still responsible for the debt. People, there is no shortcut around personal responsibility. You made the charges, so you are responsible for the debt you ran up.

Keep sending in your payments. Print a copy of the canceled check or e-payment and keep it in a safe place. Chances are the transition to your new bank will be seamless, but you never know. I think it is wise to keep a printed record for at least six months after your bank has been taken over by another bank.

SITUATION: You have a FICO credit score of 660, but you were just turned down for a car loan.

ACTION: Improve your score to 720 if you want a loan with decent terms.

As I write this in late 2009, lenders are no longer eager to lend money to people with just so-so credit. That's true of any type of loan: mortgages, car loans, private student loans. In the past (the days of irresponsible, subprime lending, circa 2007 and earlier), it was fairly easy for anyone to get a loan of any type. If you had a great FICO score (over 720), you got the best terms. But if you had a low FICO score, you could still get a loan, though you'd pay a higher interest rate and maybe higher fees. Now a low score can mean no loan. It's the same issue we have been talking about over and over: Lenders are running for safety. They are very cautious about whom they will lend to. As of late 2009, a FICO score below 700 is likely going to make it very hard to qualify for a loan, or you will have to pay a steep risk penalty: much higher interest rates and fees than you might have paid with the same score two years ago.

At some point when the financial clouds clear a bit, lenders will ease their rules and offer better terms for customers with lower FICO scores. But you and I have no idea when that will happen. I can guarantee you one thing, though: If you keep your score at 740 or better, you will always be deemed a great credit risk, no matter what mood lenders are in.

SITUATION: You want to improve your FICO credit score, but you aren't sure what to do.

ACTION: Know what matters to FICO and make the necessary changes in your financial life.

You actually have three FICO scores, one from each of the three credit bureaus: Equifax, Experian, and Trans-Union. Credit scores range from 300 to 850. A year ago, I would have told you that a score of 720 or better was all you needed to get the best loan offers. But the fallout from the credit crisis has meant that the top tier has actually been pushed higher; some mortgage lenders reserve their best rates for individuals with FICO scores above 740. Unless you plan on buying a house in the coming year, I wouldn't worry as long as your score is at least 720. That's still plenty good enough to keep most creditors happy.

If your score is below 720, here's what you need to do to make it better:

- **Pay bills on time.** This accounts for 35% of your credit score. If you are late on payments—not just credit card payments, but bills of any kind, it will pull down your score. Pay on time, even if it is just the minimum due, and it will help your score.

- **Reduce what you owe.** We already covered this earlier in the chapter. The less you owe on your cards and other debt, the less "risky" you look to potential lenders. How much you owe relative to your available credit and other debts accounts for 30% of your score.

- **Hold on to cards with a long credit history.** The longer your credit record, the more data FICO has to assess whether you are a good credit risk. This accounts for 15% of your score. Make sure you keep your card with the longest history in good shape; you don't want it to be canceled.

- **Limit your credit applications.** The more new credit you ask for, the more nervous you make lenders. New credit accounts for 10% of your FICO score. If your record shows you have applied for multiple credit cards and a new car loan at the same time, it will pull down your score.

- **Don't sweat your mix of credit.** Lenders love to see that you can responsibly handle different types of credit—for example, credit cards and a car loan and a mortgage. But your mix accounts for just 10% of your FICO score. My advice is not to pay attention to this part of the FICO scoring system. I would never recommend adding a new type of debt just to address this part of the FICO calculation. Besides, you can easily have a credit score of 740 or higher with just a few well-managed credit cards.

SITUATION: You are considering hiring a debt-consolidation company to help you with your credit card debt.

ACTION: Don't fall for the come-ons. These offers are often rip-offs and can do serious damage to your credit score and leave you in more debt than you started with.

I know how tempting it sounds when you hear an ad that tells you the Super Duper Debt Consolidation Co. is standing by to make all your credit card debt stress go away. What they don't explain is that they typically charge you 10% or so of what you owe to take on your case, and in the event they work out a settlement with your creditors, they are going to want another 10% or more of the amount they "saved" you. And I promise you, these debt-consolidation companies aren't going to spend a lot of time explaining to you that any settlement they negotiate for you will ruin your FICO credit score and may end up costing you income tax on the amount of debt that is forgiven.

Most troubling is the growing number of complaints that debt-consolidation firms collected their initial fee and then did nothing for the consumer. Not only were the clients out their fee, their FICO scores were hurt even more because the debt-consolidation firm told them they were taking care of the payments and the settlement. In reality, nothing was being done, so the amount owed ballooned as interest rates were raised and penalty fees piled up.

There is no easy way out of debt. Anyone promising to magically make everything all better is either lying to you or not explaining the financial and credit costs of what they are doing.

SITUATION: You don't know where to turn for honest help in dealing with your credit card debt.

ACTION: Contact the National Foundation for Credit Counseling. This is a network of nonprofit agencies with trained counselors who will help you assess your situation and lay out the most logical and realistic steps for you to follow. They are not miracle workers; as we just discussed, there are no miracles to be had when it comes to your credit card debt. But the NFCC are the "good guys" you can trust. Go to nfcc.org or call 800-388-2227.

SITUATION: You feel the walls caving in and fear bankruptcy is your only option.

ACTION: Contact the NFCC and get honest help in assessing your options. If you aren't eligible for a debt management plan (DMP), the counselor will try to find a workable alternative to bankruptcy. Only about 10% of their clients have ended up in bankruptcy.

That said, if in fact you owe more than what you make; if you have tried every which way to pay your bills, including working a second or even a third job; if your debt keeps growing and you are being charged 32% interest and you can't see any way out, then bankruptcy may, sadly, be an option for you. Just remember that bankruptcy will destroy your FICO credit score, but then again, if you have been behind in payments your FICO score is probably already pretty low. Bankruptcy is really a last resort when you have tried everything else. This drastic step requires the most careful consideration. You will want to find a reputable attorney who can explain the current law, the pros and cons of filing, and the different kinds of bankruptcy. For a good overview of the subject visit the credit.com website at: www.credit.com/slp/chapter8/Bankruptcy.jsp.

SITUATION: You keep getting calls saying that you owe money on a credit card, but you have no idea what the collection agency is talking about.

ACTION: First of all, verify the debt. Debt collection agencies can pursue old debts that have never been paid off, hoping you will pay money to stop the calls. But plenty of times the debts are false—the result of identity theft, clerical errors, or credit reports that have not been updated. Sometimes a debt is so old it's passed the time period when a debt collector could legally sue to collect (see below). Within 30 days of being contacted, send the collector a letter (be sure to send it certified mail, return receipt requested) stating you do not owe the money, and requesting proof the debt is valid (such as a copy of the bill you supposedly owe). If the collection agency doesn't verify the debt within 30 days, it can no longer keep contacting you and cannot list the debt on your credit report. Remember your best shot at avoiding these "zombie" debts that erroneously resurface is by staying on top of your credit report. In these credit-crunched times, no one can afford a single inaccuracy that could lower a credit score. Go to annualcreditreport.com to get your free credit report. Each of the three credit bureaus, Equifax, Experian, and Transunion, are required to provide you with one free report a year.

SITUATION: You haven't been able to pay your credit card bills for some time and your cards were shut down five years ago, but you are still getting calls saying you owe money.

ACTION: Check out your state's statute of limitations on debt collection. In every state, the statue of limitations for credit card debt begins to tick from the date you failed to make a payment that was due—as long as you never made another payment on that credit card account. (You can find the list of state statutes at www.fair-debt-collection

.com/statute-limitations.html.) One way to prove the statute applies to your debts is to get a copy of your credit report. It will list the dates you were delinquent as reported by your creditors. So if your state's statute of limitations on credit card debt is five years, and your last payment was due on April 12, the statute of limitations on that debt will run out five years from that April 12, assuming you haven't made another payment. (Please note: statutes will vary for different types of debt. The statutes of limitations are different for credit card accounts than for mortgages and auto loans.) Also important to note: If you are contacted by a collection agency and you make a promise to send in a check or you actually do send in a small amount of money, it is possible that the statute of limitations starts all over again.

SITUATION: You are being harrassed at work by calls from collection agencies.

ACTION: The Fair Debt Collection Practices Act (FDCPA) restricts tactics that debt collection agencies may use. They cannot call you at work if they know your employer prohibits such calls. Once you tell them this, they have to stop the calls; it's wise to follow up with a letter. Show you know your rights by informing them that under provision 15 of the U.S. Code, section 1692b-c, the letter constitutes formal notice to stop all future communications with you except for the reasons specifically set forth in the federal law. Collectors also cannot phone your home so often as to constitute harassment and they cannot call before 8 A.M. or after 9 P.M. You can learn more about your rights under the FDCPA at www.credit .com/credit_information/credit_law/Understanding -Your-Debt-Collection-Rights.jsp#2.

SITUATION: You start each month with the intention that you will charge only what you can pay off at the end of the month, but it never works out as planned.

ACTION: I want to be clear, if your family is dealing with a layoff or reduced income because of a furlough, I get that you may need to use credit cards to pay for some of your family's needs until you get your finances back up to full power. That's understandable. I only ask that you truly make every effort to spend carefully; what you deemed a "need" a year ago may now qualify as a "want" that your family can—and must—do without, if only until your situation stabilizes.

But if you are telling me there's no reasonable cause—such as a layoff—but you are just stuck in a cycle where you can't make ends meet, I need you (and your partner, if you are in a relationship) to take a serious look at how this is going to play out two or three years down the line. How big will those unpaid balances be? (Or more likely, how fast will the credit card companies shut you down as your balances rise?) If you can't make ends meet now, how do you expect that to change going forward? Please don't count on promotions and pay raises, or even inheritances, for that matter. Will they materialize? Maybe, maybe not. Your predicament is similar to that of homeowners in 2004–2006 who decided to take out crazy mortgages because they were betting that in a few years their houses would increase enough in value to allow them to refinance. Instead, the bubble burst, and many of those bettors are now struggling with unaffordable mortgages or, more likely, have become part of the foreclosure wave. The point is that it is very dangerous to base spending today on what you hope will play out for you tomorrow. If life doesn't follow your script, you are in for an unhappy ending.

When it comes to managing your credit cards, it's time to answer honestly whether you are in a short-term rough spot or you are using your credit to live beyond your means. If it's the latter, it's time to make some big changes. The new normal is about being realistic about what you can afford on the income you have today. Spend as you go. What you can't pay off, you shouldn't pay for in the first place.

3

Retirement

New Rules for New Times

Saving more for retirement is not merely a desirable virtue. It is an absolute necessity. The easy explanation is that you now need to save more to make up for the losses your 401(k)s and IRAs suffered during the bear market that began in 2008.

But that's only part of the story. The fuller and more honest explanation is that long before 2008 you had fallen into a series of bad habits and faulty assumptions that are at least part of the reason why you are now wondering how you will manage to retire comfortably, let alone retire period.

Faulty assumption #1: You could just save small sums because the stock market would post large gains. You expected the markets to do most of the

43

work for you. The average annual return of the S&P 500 stock index during the 1990s was 18%. At that pace your money would double every four years. That lulled you into thinking you didn't need to set aside large sums in your 401(k) and IRAs. Modest sums were just fine as long as the markets doubled every four years.

Until they didn't.

Faulty assumption #2: You could ride the massive rise in home prices to a comfortable retirement. From January 2000 through July 2006 the S&P/ Case-Shiller index of home prices in 20 metro areas more than doubled. That fed all sorts of re- tirement strategies: You anticipated that you would one day be able to downsize or do a cash- out refinance, using the excess equity to live hap- pily ever after. Or perhaps you considered tapping a home equity line of credit or reverse mortgage to pay for that dream retirement. Home sweet home, indeed.

Then that bubble burst too. As I write this in the fall of 2009, home values in many regions are down 30% or more from their inflated 2006 highs. As I explain in "Action Plan: Real Estate," I still believe home ownership is a solid long-term in- vestment, but as a home, not a retirement plan.

The New Rules for Retirement mean that nei- ther the stock market nor the real estate market will magically produce the large gains that are needed to live comfortably in retirement. Both are viable investments. Both will do just fine. But the greatest determining factor of a secure retirement is how much you will manage to save out of your paycheck. The long-term historic average annual return for the S&P 500 is about 10%, not the 18% we saw in the crazy '90s. A 10% annualized gain translates to doubling your money every seven years or so. I happen to think 10% could be a bit optimistic for stocks going forward. Combined with the reality that some of your portfolio should also be invested in less risky bonds and cash, I think it's more reasonable to base your assumptions on a long-term annualized average gain of 7% or so for your retirement accounts. That means it will double every 10 years. If the new normal is that your money might on average double every 10 years, rather than every four years, you can do the math for yourself: It will take more saving on your part to offset more moderate market returns.

You also need to face the fact that your retirement savings might be called on to support you for a very long time. Today a 65-year-old male has an average life expectancy to age 81, and a female to age 84—that's a long time for your retirement funds to take care of you. The more you can manage to save now, the lower the risk that you will run out of money later.

And what you manage to save needs to be expertly managed. Save more and save *smarter*. I have heard from so many pre-retirees who say they lost 40% or 50% or more during the depths of the bear market. The only way that could have happened is if a portfolio was 100% invested in stocks. No pre-retiree's portfolio should have been that aggressive. But many of you also suffer from the opposite malady: You have become too conservative with your retirement money, thinking it is "safe" to put all your savings in cash or bonds. It isn't. Your money will not keep pace with inflation, and that is a very serious long-term threat to your security. Even if you are 55 and expect to retire in the next 10 years, the reality is that you could live for another 30 years. The challenge is to understand that you need to commit to an asset allocation that mixes bonds for their safety and stocks for their ability to produce inflation-beating gains. Your comfort in retirement rests on getting your allocation strategy right today.

You might also want to rethink the "when" of retirement. If you have been slow to save for retirement, or if your portfolio took a big hit, there is indeed a way to work your way out of your retirement stress: stay on the job a few more years. Just adding three more years to your career will help you save more and delay the spend-down of your retirement portfolio. The new normal of retirement means that it takes work to pull it off.

What you must do

- Make sure you have the right mix of stocks and bonds in your retirement accounts given your age.
- Do not make early withdrawals or take loans from retirement accounts to pay for non-retirement expenses.
- Convert an old 401(k) to a rollover IRA so you can invest in the best low-cost funds, ETFs, and bonds.
- Consider converting a rollover IRA or traditional IRA to a Roth IRA; the converted money will then be tax-free. Just be aware of the tax due at conversion.

Your Retirement Action Plan

PLEASE NOTE: *When I refer to 401(k)s throughout this chapter, the advice is also applicable to 403(b)s and other tax-deferred accounts.*

SITUATION: You don't plan on retiring for at least 10 years, but after living through the 50% decline in stock values from late 2007 to early 2009, you've had it with stocks. You want to stop investing in the stock market, at least until you see stocks going up again.

ACTION: Resist the temptation to stop investing in stocks. If you have time on your side—and that means at least 10 years, and preferably longer, before you need money—you want to keep a large portion of your retirement money in stocks.

As noted above, the hardest part of retirement investing is staying focused on your long-term goal, rather than getting overwhelmed by what is happening day-to-day.

SITUATION: You keep hearing that the best thing you can do is to keep investing in your 401(k), but it just makes no sense to you after incurring such big losses during the financial crisis.

ACTION: If you have time on your side, and by that I mean at least 10 years until you intend to tap your retirement savings, your concern should not be so much what your retirement accounts are worth today but what they might be worth in the future.

I understand the desire to shift all your money into a stable-value fund or money market fund offered in your 401(k). But that is a short-term salve that could leave you weaker in the long run. Why? Because once you move your money out of stocks, you give up any chance to make back your losses. Sure, the stable-value fund will inch along with a 3% to 4% gain each year, but chances are that's not enough to help you reach your long-term investing goals; the return of a stable-value fund will barely keep up with the rate of inflation. If you told me your account was already large enough that simply keeping pace with inflation was all you needed, then I would be the first to say: Move everything into the stable-value fund. But that's not the situation most people are in; they need larger gains over time to build a big enough retirement pot to retire comfortably. Only stocks offer the potential for inflation-beating gains over the long term.

SITUATION: You have more than 10 years before retirement, but you just can't stand to watch your 401(k) go down. You want to put your monthly contributions in a safe place within your retirement account.

ACTION: To be financially secure when you retire requires you to look past what is happening right now—what your account is worth at this very moment—and focus instead on the actions that will pay off for you years down the line. If you have at least 10 years or more before you intend to retire, you want to make choices today that will serve you well in 2020, 2030, and 2040. And that means continuing to invest a portion of your retirement accounts in stocks, since they offer the best chance of inflation-beating gains over the long term. Notice I said long term. There is no denying that stocks can and will be volatile over short periods. But if you are patient, history tells us that over extended periods, stocks can produce the inflation-beating gains that are the key to building retirement security.

Let's walk through a simplified hypothetical example of how sticking with stocks can pay off. Let's say you invested $200 in your 401(k)'s stock fund. The share price was $20, so your $200 bought 10 shares. One month later, let's say that the share price has fallen to $10 a share. That means your $200 can buy you 20 shares.

If, however, you decided to give up on the stock market after that one month of investing and put your $200 contribution into a stable-value fund, you would still own your 10 shares and have $200 in cash in your 401(k).

On the other hand, if you decided to keep investing your $200 contribution that month into the stock fund at $10 a share, you would now have 30 shares—the 10 you bought the first month and the 20 you bought the second.

Now, for the purposes of this exercise, let's assume that the stock fund went back up to $20 a share one month after you did this.

In the first example, where you stopped investing in the stock market, your 10 shares at $20 would now be worth $200 and you would still have $200 in the stable-value fund. So in total you would have $400 in your account. You broke even.

In the second scenario, if you kept investing, you would now have 30 shares of the stock fund in your 401(k) that is now worth $20 a share. You would now have $600 in your account—a gain of $200 over what you invested.

In the first example, you are just back to where you started. In the second, you are up 50% on your money.

I realize this is an extreme example—there is no chance your stock investments will completely rebound in one month—but I wanted to make the point clearly that the right action to take over time is invest, invest, invest. As long as you have at least 10 years until you need this money, I am telling you to try to relax and have a long-term perspective when you open your statement and the value of your account has gone down. The more it goes down, the more shares you get to buy; the more shares you buy now, the bigger the payoff when the market goes back up. Please do not stop investing now. Don't change your strategy—just change your point of view.

SITUATION: Your plan is to get out of stocks while they continue to go down, then shift your money back to stocks when things get better.

ACTION: What you are trying to do is "market timing." In the short term, you may feel as if you are doing the right thing, but it will backfire on you over the long term. And retirement investing is all about the long term.

The big problem with market timing is that if you are out of the stock market, you run the very real risk that you will not be back in the market when it rallies; there is no way you will ever make up for your losses if you miss those rallies.

Listen, I get where you're coming from: It would be so great if we could sell before the markets go down and buy before the markets go back up, but it is nearly impossible to have perfect timing because there is no telling when the big rallies will come. For example, one day in an extremely wild period in October 2008, the Dow Jones Industrial Average lost nearly 700 points. Let's say you got out of stocks that day because you had had enough. Well, two trading days later the Dow Jones Industrial Average skyrocketed more than 900 points. So you missed the rally that wiped out the losses from a few days earlier. Of course, that is a very rare and dramatic example; it's not often we get such huge swings in the space of a few trading days. But the point is clear: If you try to time the markets, you risk missing out on rallies. That's exactly what happened to so many investors who bailed out of stocks in late 2008 and early 2009 as the markets were suffering severe losses. But the sidelines were a costly place to seek refuge when the stock market posted a fast and furious 60% rally beginning in the spring of 2009. If you weren't invested during that dramatic rally you lost the chance to earn back some of your bear market losses.

I know it is not fun or easy, but a long-term buy-and-hold strategy in a diversified mutual fund or exchange-traded fund (ETF) is what works best. Here's some evidence to consider:

Let's say you invested $1,000 in 1950 and then had perfect market timing and managed to miss the 20 worst months between 1950 and June 2008. Your $1,000 would have grown to more than $800,000, according to Toreador Research & Trading. But it's not as if there is some public calendar that tells us exactly when to get in and out. So let's take a look at what happens if you missed the 20 best months for stocks during that stretch—that is, you were in cash when the market rallied. Well, your $1,000 would have grown to just $11,500. If, instead, you had invested your $1,000 and left it in the market through good and bad times, you would have ended up with more than $73,000. Sure, that's a lot less than $800,000. But it's also a lot more than $11,500. Granted, none of us think in terms of a 57-year time horizon, but please know that myriad studies similar to this one come to the same conclusion over shorter time spans too. Buy and hold is the sweet spot between elusive perfect market timing and tragic poor market timing.

SITUATION: You have time on your side, but you still don't trust history this time. You just can't shake the feeling that this time is different, that buy-and-hold investing is not the way to go.

ACTION: Push yourself to keep the faith. But if at the end of the day you can't function because you are so worried, then perhaps it is best for you to get out of stocks. However, you need to understand the serious trade-off you will make.

Let's start by stripping away your emotions for a moment. My best financial advice is for you to stay invested.

Below are the 10 most recent bear markets (periods of major losses when the stock market indexes go down at least 20%) prior to 2008.

So this is not the first (or last) scary time. What's crucial to understand is that despite all those bad times, patient investors did fine. More than fine, actually. From 1950 through 2007, the annualized

BEAR MARKET	LOSS
August 1956–October 1957	−21.6%
December 1961–June 1962	−28%
February 1966–October 1966	−22%
November 1968–May 1970	−36%
January 1973–October 1974	−48.2%
September 1976–March 1978	−19.4%
January 1981–August 1982	−25.85%
August 1987–December 1987	−33.5%
July 1990–October 1990	−19.9%
March 2000–October 2002	−49.1%

Source: The Vanguard Group; Standard & Poor's

gain for the S&P 500 stock index was more than 10%. The big takeaway: There are bad times and there are good times, and history tells us that over time, the good times outweigh the bad.

So now you know my best financial advice: Stay the course. That is what I would do if it were my money. But it's not my money. It's *your* money. And no one will ever care about your money as much as you do. So if you know that the only way you can get through these tough times is to pull your money out of stocks and into a stable-value fund or a money market, then you need to do that. I just ask that you consider everything you read in this Action Plan. From a financial point of view, you are putting yourself at the risk of never making up the losses and not making big enough gains to beat inflation. Perhaps you can strike a compromise with yourself: How about you move a small percentage of your money out of stocks and into a stable-value fund? That will make it easier to get through the rocky times, but it will keep a portion of your retirement funds invested in stocks.

I respect the emotional component of investing— something that too many professionals dismiss. All I ask of you is to try as hard as you can not to let your emotions completely derail your long-term strategy. Compromise could be the ticket for you: By moving a portion of your money into a stable-value fund—say, no more than a third or so—you should be able to sleep better during volatile times without derailing your chances of sleeping well in retirement too.

SITUATION: You want to stop contributing to your 401(k), even though your company matches your contribution, so you will have more money to pay off your credit card debt.

ACTION: Don't do it. If you work for a company that matches your contribution, I don't care how much credit card debt you have or how messy your financial life may be. You cannot afford to miss out on a company match. Do you hear me?

When your employer matches a dollar of your money with a 25-cent matching contribution or gives you 50 cents for a dollar invested that is too good a deal to pass up.

SITUATION: You want to stop contributing to your 401(k) after you reach the maximum employer match so you will have more money to pay off your credit card debt.

ACTION: Do it. Once you get to the point where you have maxed out your employer's matching contribution (ask HR to help you figure out the max you need to contribute to collect the full company match), then you absolutely should stop contributing so you have more money in your paycheck to put toward pressing goals. As I explain in "Action Plan: Credit," reducing your credit card balances is not only smart, it is necessary. But you are to make paying off credit card debt your focus only if you have already taken care of building an eight-month emergency savings fund. An emergency savings fund must be your first priority; tackling credit card debt comes second on your to-do list.

SITUATION: You plan on retiring in five years and are wondering if it makes more sense to keep contributing to your 401(k) or use the money to pay off your mortgage.

ACTION: If you intend to live in your home forever, then I recommend you focus on paying off the mortgage. With one big caveat: If you get a company match on your 401(k), you must keep investing enough to qualify for the maximum employer match. That is a great deal you are not to pass up. But I wholeheartedly recommend scaling back your contribution rate just to the point of the match so that you'll have more money in your paycheck to put toward paying off your mortgage before you retire. Yes, I realize this means you will have less saved in your 401(k), but you will also need a lot less because you will no longer have a mortgage payment to deal with in retirement, and for most retirees that is the biggest income worry.

SITUATION: You can't afford your mortgage and want to borrow or withdraw money from your 401(k) to make the payments.

ACTION: Don't do it. Too many people these days are making this huge mistake. I understand that you are desperate to hang on to your house and will do anything to avoid foreclosure, but I definitely do not want you to take a withdrawal. You will pay income tax and may also be hit with a 10% penalty for money taken out before you are 59½. And then, six months later, you will find yourself back in the same hole: All the money from your 401(k) will be gone and once again you will fall behind on your mortgage.

A 401(k) loan carries a ton of risk too. If you are laid off, you typically must pay back the loan within a few months. So if you take out the loan, get laid off, and can't pay the money back ASAP, you will run into another tax problem: The loan is treated as a withdrawal and you'll be stuck paying tax—and possibly a 10% early-withdrawal penalty. A loan is also dangerous because the markets may rally during the time you have taken out the loan, which means you will have missed an important period to recoup some of your losses.

It's also important to know that money you have in a 401(k) or IRA is protected if you ever have to file for bankruptcy. You get to keep that money no matter what.

My preference is that you scour every part of your financial life to find other income sources for covering your mortgage. See "Action Plan: Spending" for advice on how to squeeze more savings out of your current income.

SITUATION: Your credit card account was closed down and your interest rate on the remaining balance was increased to 32%. You want to take a 401(k) loan to wipe out the credit card debt.

ACTION: As noted above, it is just too risky to take out a loan from your 401(k). I understand the damage a 32% credit card interest rate can do, but I want you to resist the temptation to raid your 401(k). Please review "Action Plan: Spending" for my advice on how to seriously tackle your expenses to find savings you can then put toward important financial goals, such as paying off high-rate credit card debt.

SITUATION: You've been laid off and don't know what to do with your 401(k).

ACTION: Whenever you leave a job—voluntarily or not—you have a few options for how to deal with your 401(k). If you have at least $5,000 in your account, you can leave it right where it is.

That, however, only makes sense if you have a great plan that offers great low-cost funds. If that isn't the case, I recommend you do a direct rollover into an IRA. Your money is transferred from the 401(k) into an IRA at a discount brokerage or low-cost fund family you choose. The advantage of a rollover is that you are no longer limited to your plan's lineup of funds. Once you move the money into an IRA you can choose to invest in the best low-cost mutual funds and exchange-traded funds, individual stocks, and/or bonds. *You* determine your allocation strategy. You can stick with the allocation you had in your 401(k) and roll over your money into funds, ETFs, and bonds that will re-create that mix. Or, if you weren't really following a diversified allocation strategy with your old 401(k), this is your chance to get it right.

If you are uncomfortable putting all your money into the market in one lump sum, then you can start by moving your 401(k) into a money market when you do the IRA rollover. Then from that pot you can dollar cost average: each month put one-twelfth of your money to work in the funds and ETFs you have chosen. It's a smart way to ease your money into the markets over time, thereby reducing the risk of investing 100% at the highest prices. But if you already had your money well diversified in your 401(k), there's no need to dollar cost average; I would just stay on the same path by rolling your money into the IRA following the exact same allocation strategy you were using with the 401(k).

Follow my rollover tips:

- **Never touch the money yourself.** Make sure it is a direct rollover in which your 401(k) administrator sends the money directly to the company handling your new account. If you serve as the personal go-between, you can trigger an ugly tax situation.

- **Consider converting to a Roth when you roll over.** Beginning in 2010 there is no longer an income limit on who is eligible to convert a traditional IRA into a Roth IRA. You know I think Roth IRAs are the way to go for most people; the prospect of tax-free withdrawals is compelling, especially when you consider the likelihood that we are facing higher tax rates to deal with our federal debt. When you roll over a traditional 401(k) into an IRA, you can choose to move it into a Roth IRA. (You can do this in one step: You do not need to first roll over into a traditional IRA and then convert.) Now, the one catch is that you will owe tax on the amount converted. You should consider converting only if you have money to pay for the conversion. Both Fidelity and Vanguard have easy online conversion calculators that can help you get a handle on the tax cost of converting and the potential payoff down the line. I also recommend you consult a CPA if you are considering this move.

■ **Never do a cash-out.** It is true that when you leave a job you also have the option of cashing out the value of your 401(k). That is absolutely the worst thing you can do—do you hear me? I want you to leave the money invested for your retirement—whether you keep it in the 401(k) or roll it over into an IRA. Those are your only options. Please resist the temptation to raid your retirement today. If you do that, you are jeopardizing your retirement security years from now.

SITUATION: You have been laid off and need the money in your 401(k). Can you withdraw it without paying the 10% penalty?

ACTION: Yes, if you are 55 years of age or older in the year you were laid off. You will, however, still have to pay ordinary income tax on what you withdraw. I want to be clear: I am not recommending that you take money out of your retirement accounts at such a young age, but I want you to understand your options if you find yourself in a very tough situation. Please do everything you can to avoid tapping your retirement money today. Using your savings before you retire should only be considered as a last resort.

SITUATION: You are under 55 in the year you were laid off. You desperately need the money in your retirement account just to make ends meet. Is there a way you can withdraw it without having to pay the 10% penalty?

ACTION: Yes. But it is tricky. Look into setting up a withdrawal plan that allows you to take out substantial and equal periodic payments (SEPP) from your retirement account without paying the 10% penalty. Please check with your tax advisor so he or she can tell you exactly how it works—it is covered by Rule 72t in the IRS code—and make sure your advisor is an expert in this area, because it is very complicated. This applies to all kinds of retirement accounts, not just 401(k)s and 403(b)s as the situation above does. And I need to repeat what I said above: Taking money out of your retirement account at an early age is obviously not ideal. So please do everything possible to leave your retirement money untouched.

SITUATION: You aren't working, but you still want to contribute to a Roth IRA.

ACTION: You typically must have earned income to be eligible to contribute to an IRA. The only exception is if you are married and not working but your spouse works. If that is the case, then you can make an IRA contribution through what is known as a spousal IRA: As long as your spouse has earned income that is at least equal to your IRA contribution, you are able to make the retirement investment. For example, if your spouse has at least $10,000 in earned income, you both can contribute $5,000 in 2010 to your IRAs (the maximum allowed for individuals below the age of 50; anyone 50 or older may contribute $6,000). If you are not married and have no income, you can't contribute to an IRA.

SITUATION: If I do an IRA rollover and then get another job with a company that has a great 401(k), can I put the money back into the 401(k) from the IRA rollover so it's all in one place?

ACTION: You'll need to check with your employer to see if they'll allow this, but even so, I have to tell you I think it's a bad idea. As I explain above, an IRA generally affords you greater flexibility to choose the best low-cost investments; even great company plans restrict you to a limited array of options.

SITUATION: You are worried that your company may go bankrupt and that you will lose all the money in your 401(k).

ACTION: Confirm that your money was sent from your employer to your 401(k) plan and you have nothing to worry about. Money you invest in a 401(k) is your money, not your employer's. Your employer hires a third party—typically a brokerage, fund company, or insurance company—to run the 401(k), and that company in turn segregates your money in a separate account that is all yours; even if that brokerage or fund company got into trouble.

SITUATION: You have employer matching contributions that are not fully vested and you are concerned that you may lose this money if your company goes bankrupt.

ACTION: That could indeed happen. Money that is not vested is not yet yours. So in the event your company goes under, it is not legally obligated to leave the unvested portion of your match in your account. The money *you* contribute to your 401(k) is always 100% yours.

SITUATION: Your employer has suspended making matching contributions to your 401(k). Should you keep up your contributions?

ACTION: Because you are not going to get the matching contribution, you want to be strategic about how best to use your money. If you don't have an eight-month emergency savings fund in pace, or you have credit card debt to pay off, suspend your 401(k) contributions so you have more money in your paycheck to put toward these two important financial goals. If you have no credit card debt and you have an eight-month emergency fund, then I suggest you suspend your 401(k) contributions and instead—if you qualify—invest in a Roth IRA account. If you don't qualify, invest in a traditional IRA. If you already have funded your Roth or IRA, then just keep taking that extra money to pay down the mortgage on your home if you plan to stay in that home forever or keep contributing to your 401(k); even without the company match, it remains a smart way to save tax-deferred for your retirement.

SITUATION: You have money in an old employer's 401(k) and wonder if you should leave it where it is, transfer it to your new employer's plan, or do an IRA rollover.

ACTION: Do an IRA rollover. Rather than be restricted to the handful of mutual funds offered in your 401(k), you get to pick the funds, exchange-traded funds (ETFs), and stocks or individual bonds to invest in when you do an IRA rollover. That puts you in total control and allows you to choose the best low-cost investments for your retirement money.

SITUATION: You want to do an IRA rollover, but you don't know how.

ACTION: Choose the financial institution you want to move your money to (that's the rollover part) and that company will help you switch the money from the 401(k) into your new IRA account. I believe keeping your costs as low as possible is vitally important, so I recommend discount brokerages or no-load fund companies that also have a low-cost brokerage arm for your bond and ETF investing. Once you pick the firm you want to move your money to, all you will need to do is complete an easy rollover application form and choose the option for a direct rollover; that means your new firm will contact your old 401(k) directly and get your money moved. Once your IRA is in place, set up an automated monthly investment (from a bank account) for the growth portion of your retirement portfolio. I highly recommend making monthly investments rather than big, once-a-year lump-sum investments. Periodic investments are a way to dollar cost average, a smart investment strategy for stock investing.

SITUATION: You want to do an IRA rollover but are not sure if you should roll it over into a traditional IRA or a Roth IRA.

ACTION: When you convert any money into a Roth IRA that was in either a traditional 401(k) or a traditional IRA, you will owe taxes. So you need to consider carefully how you will come up with the cash to cover a tax bill. One strategy is to convert just a small portion at a time, so you aren't hit with a staggering tax bill. I also highly recommend you consult a tax advisor with expertise in Roth conversions to make sure you choose a strategy that does not put you in a tax bind.

But here is what you need to understand: The money in your 401(k) is, in most instances, tax-deferred. That means when you eventually withdraw money from it in retirement, it will be taxed at your ordinary income tax rate. If you roll it over into a traditional IRA, the system stays the same for tax purposes.

A Roth IRA is different: You invest money that you have already paid tax on and then in retirement you get to take out all the money in your Roth without paying any tax on it. So the smart thing to do with your 401(k) is to roll it over first into an IRA rollover. Then, depending on how much money you actually have in your IRA rollover, you would either convert it to a Roth IRA little by little or do it all at once. (You also have the option of doing a direct rollover from your traditional 401(k) to a Roth IRA, with tax due on the entire conversion.) Remember, you will owe taxes on whatever amount of money you convert. (The tax on conversions made in the 2010 tax year can be paid over two years.) But if you go through this effort there is a nice payoff: The growth on the money in your Roth IRA will be tax-free if you leave it untouched until you are 59½ and have owned the Roth for at least five years. You can learn more about Roth conversions at www .fairmark.com/rothira.

SITUATION: You want to convert to a Roth IRA but were told your income is too high.

ACTION: Beginning in 2010, everyone is allowed to roll over a 401(k) or a traditional IRA into a Roth IRA regardless of income. If you convert in 2010, any tax due on your conversion can be paid over two years. The tax bill for conversions made after 2010 must be paid in one year.

SITUATION: You aren't sure if you qualify for a Roth, and how much you can contribute if you do.

ACTION: In 2010, the Roth contribution limit is $5,000 if you are under 50 years old; if you are above 50, you can invest up to $6,000. Individuals with modified adjusted gross income below $105,000 and married couples filing a joint tax return with income below $167,000 can invest up to those maximums. Individuals with income between $105,000 and $120,000 and married couples with income between $167,000 and $176,000 can make reduced contributions. Any financial institution that offers Roth IRAs will have an online calculator or a customer-service representative to help you determine your eligibility.

SITUATION: You qualify for a Roth, but you wonder why you should bother with one if you can just keep contributing to your 401(k) after you exceed the company match.

ACTION: It's important to understand that all the money you pull out of your 401(k) (or traditional IRA, for that matter) will be taxed at your ordinary income-tax rate. And given the large deficits our country faces—to say nothing of the large bills for various bailouts and stimulus projects—there is every reason to believe that tax rates are going to be higher in the future, not lower. How do you protect yourself from those higher tax rates? Invest your retirement money in a Roth IRA. If the account has been open for at least five years and you are 59½ when you take it out, it will not be taxed, period. It is far better to pay taxes on your money today so you never have to pay them again. Also, it's helpful to know that you can always withdraw any money you originally contributed to your Roth at any time, without taxes or penalties, regardless of your age. Only the growth on your contributions must stay in your Roth until you are 59½. At that point, and if the account has been open for at least five years, you'll be able to withdraw the growth tax-free as well.

Another great benefit of a Roth is that if you do not need to make withdrawals, the IRS will not force you to; you can just leave the money growing and eventually pass it along to your heirs as an amazing tax-free inheritance. That's quite different from a traditional IRA and 401(k): The IRS insists you start making required minimum distributions no later than the year you turn 70½.

SITUATION: Your income is too high to invest in a Roth IRA.

ACTION: Invest in a traditional (nondeductible) IRA and then convert to a Roth IRA, but only if you are sure you can handle the tax bill due on conversion.

SITUATION: You don't know how to invest the money you have in your retirement account.

ACTION: You need a mix of stocks and bonds; the mix is mostly a function of how many years you have until you retire, but I also respect that your "risk tolerance" might affect your decision making. In the questions that follow, I tell you what percentage of stocks and bonds you should have if you are five years from retirement, 10 to 15 years from retirement, or 20 or more years from retirement.

EXCHANGE-TRADED FUNDS (ETFs)

AND NO-LOAD MUTUAL FUNDS: *For your stock holdings, I'd like you to focus on either no-load index mutual funds, ETFs, or high-yielding, dividend-paying stocks. ETFs and no-load mutual funds are the best way to build a diversified portfolio. Each mutual fund or ETF owns dozens and often hundreds of stocks; for those of you who do not have large sums of money ($100,000 or more) to invest, that is a safer way to go than if you put all your money into a few individual stocks.*

BONDS: *I prefer you to invest in individual bonds, rather than bond funds. I'll explain below.*

SITUATION: You don't know which is better—a no-load mutual fund or an ETF?

ACTION: If your retirement account offers them, ETFs are the way to go.

Here's what you need to understand: Mutual funds and ETFs both charge what is known as an annual expense ratio. This is an annual fee that everyone pays, but it is sort of hidden in that you won't see it deducted from your account as a line-item cost; instead, it is shaved off of your fund's return. There are no-load index mutual funds that have very low expense ratios—below 0.30%. But ETFs can be even better, with annual expense ratios of as little as 0.07%. I know that sounds like a very small difference, but hey, every penny you keep in your account rather than pay as a fee is money that continues to grow for your retirement. That's just one reason why I love ETFs. The one catch with ETFs is that they trade on the stock markets as if they were a stock, so that means you will have to pay a commission to buy and sell ETF shares; when you buy a no-load mutual fund you do not pay a commission. Discount brokerages often charge $10 or so. That's not a big deal to pay a few times a year, but you sure don't want to pay that commission if you are making investments every month with small amounts of money (dollar cost averaging). If that's the case, you are better off putting money in your IRA every month into a money market account and then purchasing your ETFs every three months rather than every month. That way you save on commissions.

SITUATION: You want to invest in stocks, but you're confused by all the choices. What's a good long-term strategy?

ACTION: A solid long-term strategy for the stock portion of your portfolio is to put 70% of your stock money in a broad U.S. index fund or ETF and 30% in an international stock fund or ETF. The Vanguard Total Stock Market Index fund (VTSMX) and its ETF cousin, the Vanguard Total Stock Market ETF (VTI), are good choices for your U.S. investment. For the international portion, you can opt for the Vanguard Total International Stock Index (VGTSX) or the iShares MSCI EAFE ETF (EFA).

PLEASE NOTE: *If you are currently invested in cash or bonds, and are ready to follow my strategy for owning stocks, don't rush to move all your money into stocks in one lump sum. I recommend you use the dollar-cost-averaging strategy explained in this chapter and invest equal amounts each month over the next year to move your money slowly into stocks.*

SITUATION: You aren't sure if the fixed-income portion of your money belongs in bonds or bond funds.

ACTION: Buy individual bonds if you can, not bond funds.

I prefer bonds to bond funds because with a high-quality bond you know you will get the amount you invested back once the bond matures. For example, if you invest $5,000 in a Treasury note with a five-year maturity, you will get the $5,000 back after the note matures in five years. During the time you own the note, you will also collect a fixed interest for all of those five years. (By the way, a note works just like a bond; it's just that our Treasury likes to call them notes.) The problem with bond funds is that they do not have a maturity date and their interest rate is not fixed. So you may get back less than what you invested and your interest rate could go down over the years.

I recommend keeping the bond portion of your account in Treasuries and/or CDs if you are in a retirement account, and high-quality general-obligation municipal bonds outside of a retirement account. As I write this in late 2009, interest rates are very low, so I think it's wise to stick with notes or bonds that mature in five years or less. In the coming years, we may see higher interest rates, so I don't want you to lock up your money today for 10 years or longer. Stick with shorter maturities so you can reinvest at what I expect will be higher rates in the future. (If your money is in a 401(k) and you are five years or less from retirement, I think it is best to stick with the stable-value fund or the money market option, rather than the bond fund.)

SITUATION: You are five years away from retirement and you feel you cannot afford to lose one penny more in your 401(k) plan. What should you do?

ACTION: Ideally, you don't want to bail out of stocks completely. Let's review a few important issues. First, any money you know you will need in the next five to 10 years to pay bills does not belong in the stock market. Never has and never will. But just because you are retiring in five years, it doesn't mean you will need to use all that money immediately, right? Some you will start to use, and the rest you won't touch for 10 or 20 or even 30 years, given our longer life spans. If that sounds like your situation, I would ask you to think about keeping 25% to 30% or more of your money in stocks even if you are just five years from retirement.

If your issue is that you lost so much money you worry you won't have enough for retirement and you want to keep what you have safe, then you need to face facts. Moving all your money into a stable-value fund is not the solution. Here's what you need to do: Delay your retirement for another three years or more. That will give your stocks more time to recover. It will also potentially give you more working years to save more. And most important, it means you delay when you start to need the money; every year you can put off touching your retirement savings is going to be a tremendous help to you.

Now, the one exception here is if in fact you have determined that when you retire you want to use all your Roth IRA money to pay off your mortgage. In that case, you will indeed "need" all your money sooner rather than later. And to repeat myself: Money you know you need within five to 10 years does not belong in stocks. Put it all in your retirement plan's stable-value fund or money market account.

SITUATION: You are 10 years from retirement and you don't know how much should be invested in stocks and how much should be in bonds or cash.

ACTION: Keep at least 50% of your money in individual bonds, CDs, or stable-value funds or money market accounts. The absolute best move when you are nearing retirement is to reduce your risk, and that means moving out of stocks and into bonds. But this only makes sense if your stash at the point you retire is big enough that you can get by on it earning 4% or so a year from bond interest. You need to make sure you have a large enough amount saved up and you have figured your costs correctly to be able to move completely into bonds and live comfortably. It's also important to realize that even if you retire at 60, there's a very good chance you will live to be 80 or even 90. So you are asking your retirement fund to support you for 20 or 30 years. The simple math is that if you are making withdrawals from your retirement account each month and your remaining balance is growing at just 4% or so a year, you run the risk that your money will not last 20 or 30 years. (Just about every financial institution has a free online retirement calculator that will estimate how long your money will last. Or type "retirement calculator" into your search engine.) You need to balance the growth potential of stocks with the fact that you will soon be relying on your retirement account to live. A 50-50 mix is a good target for balancing those two different needs.

As I explain later in this chapter, I think ETFs that focus on dividend-paying stocks are a very smart place for your stock investments today. The income you receive from the dividend is a good way to "get paid" today while still investing in stocks for future gains. If you currently have a 50% stock investment and want to invest in dividend-paying stocks, you can make the switch over. If, however, you have a lot of money in bonds or cash, please take your time moving money into a stock ETF; rather than one lump-sum investment, make smaller monthly investments—known as dollar cost averaging—over the course of the next year.

SITUATION: You don't plan to touch your retirement money for 10 to 15 years. How much should be invested in stocks and how much should be in bonds/cash?

ACTION: If you have 15 years until retirement, have about 70% in stocks and then scale that back by 5 percentage points or so each year, so that when you are 10 years from retirement you have 50% in stocks.

SITUATION: You have 20 or more years until retirement and you want to know how much should be invested in stocks and how much should be in bonds/cash.

ACTION: Aim for 80% to 100% stocks. You are in a great situation. You have so much time on your hands that you can ride out this bear market and profit when the market rallies.

If you are afraid to have all your money in the

market, there is nothing wrong with keeping 20% or so in bonds/cash. With that mix, you are going to do well when the stock markets rally and also have a nice bond cushion to reduce your portfolio's losses when the stock market is falling. If that helps you relax a bit and stay committed to a long-term strategy, I think 20% in bonds is just fine, but I'd prefer to be in stocks 100%.

SITUATION: You were planning on retiring in the next few years, but after seeing your portfolio take a big drop during the bear market, you're not sure you can still afford to.

ACTION: Focus on what the market loss will mean to you in terms of monthly income.

Let's say in 2007 you had a $250,000 retirement stash. Today it is $200,000. So what does that mean to you in terms of retirement income? Your intention at retirement was to have your money invested mostly in bonds so your money would be safe and you could count on a return of approximately 4%. The $50,000 you lost would generate $2,000 in income at a 4% rate. In other words, your real monthly loss in income comes to about $170 a month. So the question is, does that loss of $170 a month mean you can no longer retire? If the answer to that question is yes, then the truth is you really were cutting it too close to retire anyway.

The best move you can make is to delay your retirement, even by just a few years. The more time you give your portfolio to recover, and the fewer years you will rely on that portfolio to support you in retirement, the better shape you will be in. If you can keep saving for retirement during those extra few years you work, that will obviously help too. But even if you decide to take a less stressful job that does not pay as much as you currently earn—and you find it harder to save for retirement—you are still doing yourself a world of good. Every year you can live off of earned income is a year you are not requiring your retirement savings to support you. Now, I am not suggesting that you work until you are 80. But if you have set your sights on an early retirement at 60 or 62, I want you to consider working to 65 or maybe even 70, even if only part-time. Don't look at it as punishment. It is an opportunity to live a less-stressful life, because you are not going to stretch yourself too thin. I also want you to focus on the fact that our average life expectancy keeps getting longer and longer. A 65-year-old man today has an average life expectancy to age 81, and a 65-year-old woman has a 50-50 chance of living to 84.5 years of age. That means many of us will be asking our retirement savings to support us for many years; by continuing to work until at least your mid- to late 60s, you will reduce the pressure on your savings to support you later on.

SITUATION: You are retired and need more income to make ends meet. You wonder if a reverse equity mortgage is a solution to your shortfall.

ACTION: A reverse mortgage can indeed be a good solution, but you must understand how it works. There are some serious trade-offs to making this choice that you should be aware of.

With a reverse mortgage, the roles are, well, reversed. Instead of you paying a lender, a lender pays you a sum based on the value of your home, your age, and interest rates at the time you take out the loan. You can be paid each month, you can take out all the money in a lump sum, or you can set up a line-of-credit account from which you withdraw money as you need it. (Or you can opt for a mix of all those options.) In 2010 the upper limit for an FHA-insured reverse was $625,500.

There is no risk you will lose your house if you do a reverse. You can stay in the home as long as you like, but when you move or die, the bank that owns the reverse gets repaid. Typically that involves selling the home. If the home sells for more than the value of the reverse, your heirs receive the excess. But if the sale price does not cover the value of the reverse, your heirs will not be on the hook. The bank can never collect more than the home's value at the time of the sale.

You must be at least 62 years old to take out a

reverse mortgage. If you are married you both must be at least 62, or you can opt to remove the younger spouse from the title.

I do not recommend a reverse if you intend to move in a few years anyway, because the fees on these loans can be very expensive. You will pay an origination fee of 2% on the first $200,000 and then 1% on the balance above $200,000, up to a maximum of $6,000 for the total origination fee. Most reverse mortgages are insured by the FHA— the FHA refers to these loans as Home Equity Conversion Mortgages (HECM)—and that means there is an insurance premium attached; it amounts to an additional up-front 2% and an annual premium of 0.5%. You'll also be hit with closing costs on the loan, including an appraisal. All told, fees can easily be 8% to 10% of your loan amount. If you plan on staying in your home for many years, those fees can be worth it. What's not wise is taking out a reverse when you anticipate moving in a few years.

The AARP website (www.aarp.org/revmort) has a special section that walks you through the basics and has valuable information on how to recognize any offers that are too good to be true. Sadly, there is no shortage of con artists out there looking to take advantage of the elderly. There is also great information available from the Department of Housing and Urban Development, which oversees the FHA reverse program. Go to www

.hud.gov and type HECM into the search box. You can use a free online calculator to estimate how much you may receive through an FHA-insured reverse mortgage.

SITUATION: You have an IRA at a brokerage firm, but you're worried that if the company goes under, you will lose all your money.

ACTION: Stop worrying. The money you have invested in your accounts at a brokerage or fund company is completely separate from the operations of the parent company. The brokerage or fund company can't use your money to pay its bills and debt.

Even if a company goes under, what happens is that you will transfer your money to another brokerage or fund company. Or, more likely, the company will be taken over and you become a client of that new company.

And just so you know, if there is an irregularity and a company uses your money fraudulently, you may be able to recover up to $500,000 ($100,000 limit for cash accounts) from the Securities Investor Protection Corp. This is not like federal insurance. It's a voluntary program of member firms that keeps a kitty around to settle problems; at the end of 2008, SIPC had about $1.7 billion in its fund. This covers standard investment accounts only; SIPC does not cover alternatives such as currency and commodity investments. Check with your brokerage or fund company to see if it belongs to SIPC.

SITUATION: You have a variable annuity and are worried that the insurance company will go under and you will lose all your money.

ACTION: Money invested in a variable annuity is typically in segregated subaccounts that are separate from your insurer's balance sheet. Even if the insurer runs into trouble, your money should not be affected. Now, that said, you do need to understand that your variable annuity is susceptible to market losses; that's what the word "variable" means. How much your account is worth is largely a function of the performance of the subaccounts (funds) you are invested in.

SITUATION: You have a single-premium fixed annuity and are worried that the insurance company will go under and you will lose your money.

ACTION: With a single-premium fixed annuity your payout is indeed a guarantee from your insurer, so if your insurer goes under there is reason to be concerned. Concerned, but not panicked.

First, in the unlikely event anything happens to your insurer, there is a state guaranty fund that will swoop in to cover annuity payments—up to certain limits. In most states, the guaranteed payout for an annuity is $100,000, though it can be higher in some states. (Go to www.nohlga.com and use the locator to find your state's insurance department, where you can learn about your state's guaranty fund limits.)

If your annuity exceeds your state's guaranty limit, you need to weigh the cost of cashing out carefully.

SITUATION: You are retired and need a higher income payout than you can get from bank CDs today.

ACTION: Consider municipal bonds and dividend-paying stock mutual funds or ETFs.

I want to be clear: You never want to put money that is in an IRA, 401(k), or other tax-deferred account in municipals. Because your money is already tax-deferred, you get no added benefit from buying munis. So I am talking about money you invest outside of your IRA and 401(k). Now, I know that earlier I told you that the bond portion of your IRA and 401(k) should be kept in Treasuries with short maturities, but I have a different strategy for municipal bonds. I think it is smart to invest in municipal bonds with maturities of 10 to 20 years. In the fall of 2009, a 20-year general-obligation municipal bond had a yield of 4.4%. For someone in the 28% federal tax bracket, that is the equivalent of a 6.1% yield. That is a seriously great return on your money. If you are in a higher tax bracket, your return will be even higher.

As much as I love municipal bonds, I want to emphasize that this strategy only makes sense if you have at least $100,000 to invest; that is how much you need to be able to buy a diversified portfolio of five to 10 different bonds and not be hit with outrageous fees. You need to be particularly strategic these days, given the financial pressure many states and municipalities are under. I recommend sticking with General Obligation (GO) municipal bonds rather than revenue bonds (in which your payout is dependent upon the income generated by the project being financed by the bond). If you live in a state with big budget woes, it might be wise to add a few out-of-state bonds from more stable states. Yes, you may have to pay income tax on the payouts from out-of-state bonds, but having a well-diversified portfolio is more important in this environment than avoiding tax on every dollar you invest.

Another strategy to generate more income is to invest a portion of your money in high-dividend individual stocks or ETFs. The dividend payout from stocks can be a valuable income stream.

However, you need to know that dividend stocks of course have greater risk than a bank CD. Even though you are receiving a dividend payout, the underlying value of your shares can indeed fall. And there is always the possibility that some companies might find that they have to suspend or reduce their dividend payout if they hit a severe rough patch. Indeed, according to Standard & Poor's, in the second quarter of 2009, 250 companies decreased their dividend payouts, the worst stretch for dividend-paying stocks in more than 50 years. You need to understand that companies choose to pay dividends—they are not required to do so.

So here's my strategy for cautious dividend investing:

- Invest only money that you know you will not need to cash in for at least the next 10 years. You will earn income (the dividend payout) on the money, but because these are stocks, you want to know that if the share price declines you won't have to sell at a big loss.

- Stick with low-cost ETFs. Owning individual stocks increases your risk of suffering big losses if there is an unexpected problem in that one company or industry. It's safer to invest in a diversified portfolio of dividend-paying stocks. I like Vanguard High Dividend Yield (VYM) and iShares Select Dividend Index (DVY) if you invest in ETFs.

4

ACTION PLAN

Saving

New Rules for New Times

There is no substitute for having an emergency savings account safely tucked away at a federally insured bank or credit union.

None. Do you hear me?

Credit card: no substitute.

HELOC: no substitute.

Money market mutual fund: not a 100% guarantee either.

Notion of job security: I need you to pay attention: Even corporate rock stars got laid off in the recent recession. I don't care how talented and beloved you are at the office, you can't tell me that there is zero risk you could be laid off, handed a pay cut, or face an income-pinching furlough.

The New Rules for Saving require you to have real money tucked away at a real federally insured bank or credit union. That is the only way you can be certain that you will be able to handle any of life's unexpected "what ifs" and "uh-ohs." I have always advocated the necessity of having a real emergency savings fund, but now more than ever, I hope you can see for yourself the dangers of relying on a credit card or HELOC when what you really need is fast cash for an emergency.

Not only must you have a bona fide savings account at a federally insured bank or credit union, you need to fund it to the point where it can support your family for up to eight months. Yes, I said eight months. Yes, I know that is a long time and a lot of money. But don't try to tell me that is an unreasonable scenario. You need to appreciate that eight months is what it realistically takes to truly protect you and your family. If you are laid off it can take awhile to find your next job; as I write this in the fall of 2009, the average time to land a new job is six months. If you are facing a furlough or a year without a bonus, or if, God forbid, someone in your family falls ill, you handle all of that by knowing you have an emergency reserve you can tap.

I recognize it may take you months, perhaps even a few years, to fill your emergency fund up to my eight-month requirement. The call to action is that you must start saving—or saving more—today. Not tomorrow. Not next month. Today.

You also need to understand how to keep your savings safe. That starts by making sure your bank or credit union is part of the federal insurance program that guarantees repayment of every penny deposited no matter what happens to the institution. Through 2013, up to $250,000 per person is fully insured at participating banks and credit unions; you can qualify for even more coverage depending on the types of accounts you have.

Safety also comes from prudent investment choices. As of fall 2009, bank savings and CD accounts offer yields of 1%, 2%, or maybe 3% if you're lucky. Not much, I know. But listen to me, there is no choice in this matter: You must keep the money safe. Do not move your emergency savings into the stock market in search of higher returns. You do not chase higher returns with your emergency account; you keep it safe and sound.

My hope is that once you build up your emergency savings to the point where it can support your family for eight months, you will make it a permanent piece of your financial portfolio. There will indeed be a time when the credit markets shift and once again credit card limits will be expanded and offers of HELOCs will be extended. That shouldn't be an excuse to drain your emergency savings and revert to using these quasi emergency funds. That's just too risky. I can guarantee that at some point in the future we will once again run into a period when the credit markets retrench. Let's hope it won't be triggered by an economic downturn on par with what we experienced in recent years. But the economy is cyclical; there will always be ups and downs. Having a permanent emergency savings stash is how you insulate yourself from the inevitable economic downturns and buy yourself protection for any of life's unexpected and unpleasant surprises.

What you must do

- Make sure your bank or credit union is covered by federal deposit insurance.
- Check that what you have on deposit is eligible for full insurance coverage in the unlikely event your bank or credit union fails. Through December 31, 2013, the general limit has been raised to $250,000 from its previous $100,000, but you need to understand the ins and outs.
- If your savings is in a money market mutual fund sold through a brokerage or mutual fund firm, consider moving your money into the Treasury money market fund at that company.
- Build up your savings to cover eight months of living expenses.
- Move all money you need within the next five to 10 years into savings. Money you need soon does not belong in the stock market.

Your Savings Action Plan

SITUATION: You don't know if your bank or credit union is backed by federal insurance.

ACTION: Confirm that your bank is part of the Federal Deposit Insurance Corp. (FDIC) program or that your credit union is part of the National Credit Union Administration's insurance fund (NCUA). You can check a recent statement or swing by the bank or credit union. If you see the FDIC or NCUA insurance logos displayed anywhere on a statement or front door, you are halfway home. Another option is to go to www .myfdicinsurance.gov or www.ncua.gov and use the online tools to confirm that where you save is indeed backed by federal insurance.

SITUATION: You don't know if all of your money on deposit at the bank or credit union is covered by insurance.

ACTION: Prior to the credit crisis, each individual had a base guarantee of up to $100,000 per bank. So if you had a checking account, a CD, and a money market, all the accounts were fully insured if their combined total did not exceed $100,000. If you had a joint account, you and the person you shared the account with were eligible for another $100,000 each of coverage. (The same limits applied for federally insured credit unions.)

The limit for banks and credit unions was raised to $250,000 per person per bank/credit union for 2009, and this higher coverage amount has been extended through 2013. If you have less than $250,000 at any single bank or credit union and that bank or credit union is federally insured, stop worrying. You are fine through 2013.

SITUATION: Given that the $250,000 limit is in place through 2013 (it may be extended past that date, but there is no guarantee), you want to know if it is smart to invest $250,000 in a high-rate five-year CD your bank is offering.

ACTION: No. You have to understand that currently the $250,000 insurance is good only through December 31, 2013. It may be renewed past 2013, but as of now, we do not know if it will be extended. If you have more than $100,000 at one bank the safest move is to limit your CD purchases to issues that mature before December 31, 2013. That way, if for some reason the insurance coverage reverts to $100,000 in 2014, you will have the flexibility to spread your money among different banks without incurring any early-withdrawal penalties on your CDs.

To be absolutely safe, limit the money you deposit at any one bank to $100,000 or stick with a CD that expires by December 31, 2013.

SITUATION: You already purchased a long-term CD for more than $100,000 that expires after 2013, and now you're worried about what will happen if the limits are rolled back to $100,000 in 2014.

ACTION: If the limit is reduced to $100,000—and I am not suggesting this is likely, but only a possibility—you can still choose to cash in your CD early. Most banks will dock you with a penalty for an early withdrawal, but it is typically limited to forfeiting some of your interest, not principal.

SITUATION: You have more than $250,000 at one bank and are worried your money isn't 100% covered by FDIC insurance.

ACTION: You may still have full insurance coverage, but you need to check that your accounts meet the obscure rules that extend your insurance past the basic $250,000. The quickest and best way to make sure your accounts are fully insured is to go to www.myfdicinsurance.gov and plug your bank info into the easy-to-use calculator. In just a few simple steps you will have verification straight from the FDIC if all your accounts are fully insured. (Credit union members should use the

NCUA Calculator at http://webapps.ncua.gov/ins/). If you don't have easy access to a computer, I recommend marching down to your bank or credit union and having them go online with you to verify the level of coverage you have; don't just take a teller's word for it. You want to see your account information plugged into the EDIE tool (at a bank) or the NCUA Calculator (for a credit union).

SITUATION: You worry that the FDIC or NCUA will run out of money if things get really bad and there are lots of failures. You fear the insurance really isn't going to be there if and when you need it.

ACTION: Rest assured your money is safe as long as it is covered by federal insurance. That insurance is backed by the full faith and credit of the United States government. Please don't get worked up if you hear or read ominous stories that the insurance funds are running short of money. Here's the big picture to stay focused on: The FDIC and NCUA can go directly to the Treasury to get any money they need to fulfill their stated insurance promises. And the Treasury will raise any extra money it may need to cover losses that exceed what is already set aside in the insurance funds. There is absolutely no way our government is going to let depositors with insured accounts lose a penny. That promise is one of the pillars of our financial system.

SITUATION: You worry that if your bank or credit union fails, your account will be frozen and you won't be able to pay your bills or get cash out.

ACTION: Relax. Typically, when a bank or credit union is taken over by regulators it occurs on a Friday and by Monday everything is open and running as if nothing happened. It is in the best interests of the regulators to make sure depositors have quick access to their money. That's not only "good business," it is also how the regulators prevent a panicked run on the banks.

SITUATION: Your money is at a credit union and you are wondering if you should move it to an FDIC-insured bank.

ACTION: As long as your credit union belongs to the National Credit Administration's insurance fund (NCUA), your money is safe. The coverage limits and government backing are the same as those at an FDIC-insured bank. There is no need to move your money.

SITUATION: You have money deposited with an on-line bank and wonder if it is safe.

ACTION: Check if the online bank says it is part of the FDIC insurance program. Every bank that is in the FDIC insurance program—whether on-line or "bricks and mortar"—is safe. You can check the home page of your online bank; all banks that participate in the program will adver-tise that fact boldly. But I think it is smart to double-check directly with the FDIC; go to www .myfdicinsurance.gov to verify you are protected, and confirm that every penny is in fact insured.

SITUATION: A stock mutual fund you bought at your bank had a big loss in the bear market. The bank is FDIC insured, so you thought your money was safe.

ACTION: You need to understand that FDIC in-surance does not cover investments, such as a stock fund. Federal insurance for banks and for credit unions covers deposit accounts, not invest-ment accounts. A deposit account can be a check-ing, savings, CD, or money market account. But banks are also allowed to sell investments. Mutual funds are investments. Stocks and exchange-traded funds (ETFs) you buy through a bank are investments. And they have zero insurance. Zero. When you opened the account you probably signed some sort of acknowledgment that you understood this, but those disclosures are easy to miss. And, of course, there was no guarantee that your friendly bank account manager who was excited to have you make the investment took the time to slowly and clearly spell things out.

When you invest in the stock market—whether it be through a fund you buy at a bank, a credit union, a brokerage, or a fund company—you have no protection against bear market losses.

SITUATION: Last time I checked, my savings account had an interest rate of 5%, but now it is below 2%. Should I move to a bank offering accounts with higher yields?

ACTION: It is always smart to shop around for the best-yielding savings accounts, but you need to understand that banks peg the savings rate they offer consumers to the Federal Reserve's Federal Funds Rate. In the wake of the recent financial crisis the Federal Reserve aggressively cut the Federal Funds Rate. As I write this in late 2009, the Federal Funds Rate is below 0.25%. So if you are earning more than 1% or so on a regular savings account, that's actually pretty good. I am all for moving your money to the highest-yielding bank accounts, and you can check websites such as www.bankrate.com for banks that offer the highest savings rates. But if you have a competitive yield right where you are and it is FDIC insured, I wouldn't make it a huge priority to hunt for an extra 0.25% in yield. But hey, if you have the time and energy to shop around, go for it. Just remember: Only put your money in a bank that is FDIC insured or a federally insured credit union.

SITUATION: Your savings are in a money market mutual fund your broker told you was safe, but you wonder if it's as safe as an account at an FDIC-insured bank.

ACTION: The short answer is no. A money market mutual fund (MMMF) sold by a brokerage firm or a mutual fund firm is not backed by permanent federal insurance. Only a money market deposit account (MMDA) sold through a federally insured bank or credit union, or a bank subsidiary of a brokerage or mutual fund company, is eligible for insurance.

I know, I know: MMDA, MMMF—why do they have to make it all so confusing?

So just to be sure you have it down straight:

MMDA: *Sold at a bank or credit union, or through a bank subsidiary of a brokerage or fund company. Eligible for federal deposit insurance.*

MMMF: *Sold through a brokerage firm or mutual fund company. No insurance.*

Now, in normal times, an MMMF is considered just as safe as an MMDA. And for decades they were indeed just as stable as an MMDA. But in late 2008 one money market mutual fund ran into trouble because it owned a security issued by Lehman Brothers. When Lehman went bankrupt, the value of that security fell to zero and the money market fund was unable to maintain its stable $1 share value.

Here's my safe and sound MMMF strategy: Keep your money with the same firm but move it into the Treasury MMMF (every major brokerage and fund company has this option). If your money is invested in U.S. Treasuries, you have nothing to worry about. Your money is backed by the full faith and credit of the U.S. government. There aren't going to be any defaults in that portfolio. If you don't have a Treasury MMMF option at your existing brokerage or fund company, then I would consider moving my money into an insured bank deposit, or to a brokerage or fund company that offers a Treasury MMMF. (To be extra safe, I recommend that money you need to pay bills, etc., be moved into a bank or credit union MMDA account. The money market mutual fund that ran into trouble froze investor accounts and then doled out payments in small increments over many months. You need to make sure that money you need quick access to is in fact available. The only way you can guarantee you will have ready access is with an insured bank or credit union account.)

SITUATION: You understand why it makes sense to have eight months of living expenses set aside in an emergency savings fund, but there is no way you can ever save that much.

ACTION: I am well aware how stretched you are financially. I fully expect that many of you may not be able to flip the switch and magically have a bank account that is stuffed with enough money to cover eight months of living expenses. But you must start moving toward that goal. Month by month you must build security for yourself and your family. You may get to the eight-month goal in six months of aggressive saving, or it may take you a few years. That's okay. The point is that you are moving in the right direction. Every month you will have more security, not less. Check out "Action Plan: Spending" for steps on how to reduce your expenses so you have more money to put toward goals such as this one.

One of the best ways to get on a consistent savings pattern is to set up an automated deposit from your checking account into a savings account. Studies show that once you automate you tend to stick with it; that's true of bank savings accounts and your 401(k) investing. As the saying goes, set it and forget it.

Now, how much should you have deposited each month? Here's the goal. Decide how much you can afford to deposit. Now add 20% to that amount. Don't cheat here. If you were going to set aside $100 a month, commit to $120. If you were going to aim for $500 a month, it's now $600 a month. Will that be hard? Yes. Will it take some serious spending cuts? Probably. But you cannot afford to be laid back and do what is easy. You must push yourself as hard as possible to build your security as quickly as possible.

SITUATION: You are retired and need safe income, but you can't live off of 2.5% interest in your bank CDs. What are you supposed to do?

ACTION: Keep some of your money in the bank, no matter how low the yield. You must keep your savings safe. I also recommend checking out municipal bonds; as I write, you can get yields of more than 4% on bonds with 15-year maturities. That's a good deal right now and it does not require you take on the risk of investing in longer-term issues. And please check out my dividend stock strategy in "Action Plan: Retirement." It may be a smart way for you to earn more income on a small portion of your money that you're comfortable investing in the stock market.

SITUATION: You have a mortgage or a car loan with a bank that failed and you wonder if you need to keep paying it.

ACTION: You must keep paying. A bank's failure does not excuse you from paying your loan.

Very soon after a bank failure, you should receive notice of the bank that has taken over your account. And if all goes well, you will just keep paying exactly as you have, with no disruption.

Now, that said, I want you to keep very careful records of all your payments. If you use online banking, print out each payment for at least six months and tuck them away in a safe place. As I said, the transition should be seamless, but when Bank A takes over Bank B, sometimes the wires can get crossed in the back office during the switchover. So you want to have perfect records to prove any problem is not because you fell behind on payments. If you do receive a notice that you haven't paid, you have to not only deal with the bank but check your credit reports (go to www .annualcreditreport.com; you are entitled to one free credit report a year from each of the three credit bureaus) to make sure the bank has not mistakenly reported your loan payment as late or delinquent. If it is showing up on your report, you must ride the bank hard to correct the mistake. At the same time, file a dispute with the credit bureau. By law, they must look into the matter and report back to you within 30 days. Don't take anyone's word that they will take care of it. You must stay on top of the issue and keep checking (and nudging) to make sure any mistake is cleared up. As I discussed in "Action Plan: Credit," no one can afford to let their FICO credit score drop. Especially when your bank is the one that has tripped up.

5

Spending

New Rules for New Times

A welcome outcome of the financial crisis is that it has made very plain the need to return to the values of acting responsibly when it comes to your money. You now understand why it is important to have an emergency savings fund at a federally insured bank or credit union. You now know you need to shift your retirement savings into high gear. You now truly appreciate the urgency of getting out from under the credit card industry and paying off your balances once and for all.

Finally, you get it.

But you have no idea where you will get the money to put toward your newfound financial goals. Many households are grappling with a lay-off. In others, a furlough or a disappearing bonus is squeezing the family finances. Just when you have all the motivation in the world to take control of your future and build security, it's as if the universe is conspiring against you and making it doubly challenging.

There's no easy solution here. If you aren't making more, you need to create more by spending less. I know many of you are already committed to that fact. Over the past year the national savings rate has increased from less than 1% to more than 4%. It wasn't a flush paycheck that made that possible. It was your own determination to make more out of what you have. There's only one way to do that: *spend less.*

If you are one of those people who've started saving more, good for you. Now just keep it up. The New Rules for Spending say less is more. The less you spend, the more money you will have available to buy the most valuable commodity of all: security.

Don't tell me spending less is unpatriotic. I've heard that from some of you recently. Yes, I am fully aware that roughly two-thirds of our Gross Domestic Product (GDP) is based on consumer spending. I appreciate how important the consumer is to our nation's economic health. But come on—look at where all of that consumer spending has gotten us. An economy that relies on its citizens to overspend is at its core unhealthy and unsustainable. It is nonsense to suggest that to keep the economy growing you must keep spending.

Personal accountability is job one. And there is value in your saving; that money will find its way back into the system. Money you save is money that is available for investment by the institution where you place your deposits. Of course we still need a vibrant consumer to help our economy, but we also need a consumer who is committed to saving too.

The challenge now is to rethink, retool, and reimagine your budget so there is more money left over each month to put toward your newfound financial goals. It is not just scouring the bills for savings, though that's laudable; it may require downshifting your entire lifestyle to a more affordable level.

That's not punishment. On the contrary, it is freedom, my friends. Figure out how to live on less, find ways to save more, and you will be emancipated from the shackles of financial stress. Isn't that all the motivation you need?

What you must do

- Separate wants from needs.
- Get over your guilt that you aren't "providing" for your kids.
- Strike the word "deserve" from the conversation. What you deserve is irrelevant; what you can truly afford is all that counts.
- Try to negotiate better terms on a car loan you can't keep up with.

■ Be very careful when asked to cosign any loan,
  no matter how much you love the person who is
  asking for your help.

Your Spending Action Plan

SITUATION: You know your family needs to save
more, but you have no idea where to start.

ACTION: Get a grip on where your money is going. You can't move forward building an honest financial life if you don't first understand where you
are today. I want you to slowly and carefully fill out
the Household Cash Flow worksheet below. To do
this, you need to first pull out a year's worth of
bank statements and credit card statements. The
amount you put in the right-hand column should
be the average cost for the past 12 months.

  WEBSITE ALERT: *A more extensive version of
this worksheet is available for download on www.suze
orman.com.*

EXPENSES	MONTHLY COST
HOME	
MORTGAGE/RENT	
HOME EQUITY LOAN	
PROPERTY TAX	
INSURANCE	

EXPENSES	MONTHLY COST
MAINTENANCE	
UTILITIES	
Gas and Electric	
Heating	
Water	
Home Phone	
Cellphone	
Cable/TV	
Internet	
MAINTENANCE	
Repairs/Upgrades	
Gardener	
Snow Removal	
TOTAL MONTHLY HOME EXPENSES:	_____
FOOD	
Groceries	
Dining Out/Takeout	
Coffee	
TOTAL FOOD:	_____
CAR/TRANSPORTATION	
Car Loan #1	
Car Loan #2	
Gas	
Maintenance	

EXPENSES	MONTHLY COST
Tolls/Paid Parking	
Car Insurance (total all cars)	
Public Transportation	
TOTAL CAR COSTS:	

OTHER INSURANCE

Health Insurance*	
Life Insurance*	
Disability Insurance*	
Long-Term-Care Insurance*	
Dental Insurance*	
TOTAL OTHER COSTS:	

MISC. SPENDING

Child Care	
Private School Tuition	
Entertainment (Movies, DVD Rentals, Concerts, Sporting Events)	
Hair/Manicures/Pedicures	
Club Memberships	
Computer Equipment and Games	
Clothes	
Gifts	
Vacations	
Medical Copays and Out-of-Pocket Expenses	

*If these items are taken out of your paycheck, they do not need to be itemized on this worksheet, which tallies expenses against take-home pay.

EXPENSES	MONTHLY COST
Pet (Food and Vet)	
Media Subscriptions (Newspapers, Magazines, Online)	
Charitable Contributions	
Other	
Other	
Other	
TOTAL MISC. SPENDING:	
OTHER LOANS/DEBT	
Credit Card 1	
Credit Card 2	
Credit Card 3	
Student Loan	
401(k) Loan	
Bank/Personal Loan	
TOTAL OTHER DEBTS:	
MONTHLY SAVINGS/TAX PAYMENTS	
Emergency Savings Account	
401(k) Contribution*	
IRA Contribution	
College Savings Fund	
Self-Employment Tax Payments	
TOTAL SAVINGS/TAX PAYMENTS:	
TOTAL EXPENSES (A):	

INCOME	MONTHLY AMT.
After-Tax Pay	
Rental Income	
Dividend/Interest Income	
Social Security	
Retirement Income (401(k), IRA, and Pension)	
TOTAL INCOME (B):	
TOTAL INCOME–TOTAL EXPENSES (B–A):	

SITUATION: Your expenses are more than your income.

ACTION: Circle every expense in your worksheet that is a "want." It is imperative to separate expenses that are for true needs (health insurance, the electricity bill) from those that are not crucial for your family to function (gym membership, new clothes, computer games, etc.).

If you do not have an eight-month emergency savings fund, if you have credit card debt, and if you are not saving for retirement, you have no choice but to reduce and even eliminate many of the "wants" your family is spending money on.

This is not supposed to be a comfortable or easy exercise. Cutting down from four manicures a month to three is not going to get you where you need to go. Your financial security is buried in those expenses. The more you are willing to curtail spending on those expenses, the more money you have to protect your family. The $25 you don't mindlessly shell out to the kids every week when they head out to spend time with friends is $100 a month you have to put toward a term life insurance policy that protects them if anything were to happen to you. The $300 a month you don't spend on the second (or third) car your family can do without is your future retirement security; put that much in a Roth IRA for 20 years and you will have more than $157,000, assuming your money grows at an annualized 7% rate.

SITUATION: You feel guilty cutting back on what you've always provided for your family.

ACTION: Decide once and for all if you want to indulge or protect your family.

It really is that simple. If you have credit card debt and no emergency savings, I have to tell you, you do not care about your family's safety and security. All you care about is being the hero who doesn't say no, the bottomless ATM for every desire, expectation, and wish your family has.

That is indulgent. And destructive. Let's walk through this together. You look at your expense and income worksheet, get frustrated, and decide to just continue down the path of overspending. You ignore the fact that your credit card balance keeps rising. You ignore the fact that you have no emergency savings. You ignore the fact that you have very little saved up for retirement. You ignore the fact that you don't have health insurance because it is just too expensive.

And then you get laid off. Or you get sick. You can't pay the mortgage, and you have no savings to help you in this time of emergency. So the downward spiral begins. You might even lose your home. All because you feel as if you must always give your kids everything they want—and right now. How does that indulge your kids?

Or let's look even further into the future. Twenty years from now, your little ones are going to be adults, working to make ends meet for their own families. Then you come knocking on the door saying you can't afford to support yourself in retirement because you never saved up enough during your prime working years, the years when you made the decision to give your kids everything they wanted. How does that indulge your adult kids?

I appreciate that it may initially be hard to institute new financial priorities and habits in your family. Change is always a process that takes getting used to. But the real problem here is that you think acting responsibly with your money will be punishment for your kids. You think that by slowing down the spending you are taking something away from them. I couldn't disagree more. I see it as protecting them. When you make the commitment to spend less, you will have more money to put toward what your family needs: lasting financial security.

And I have to tell you: How receptive will your kids be to the change comes down to how you sell it. If you are moping, if they can feel your guilt, they are going to feel lousy. Your kids don't deserve that.

Children are incredibly adaptable, and they are going to take their cues from you. So don't pitch this as a scary time and don't suggest that they are in any way to blame for your problems. In an age-appropriate manner, let them know that you are all going to be fine, but you need to be extra careful with spending and saving to make sure the family is safe during these challenging times. For more advice about how to talk to your kids about money, read "Action Plan: Kids and Money."

SITUATION: Even after removing the "wants," you still don't have money to put toward paying off your credit card debt and building savings.

ACTION: Look for ways to pay less for your needs. You need a phone, but do you need a home phone and a cellphone? Does your family need the super-deluxe cell plan that lets everyone aimlessly text to their heart's delight, or might you be able to spend $50 less a month with a scaled-back plan? Have you really, seriously done everything to reduce your utility bills? I am talking about the low-hanging fruit of inexpensive insulation, unplugging unused electronics, replacing burned-out bulbs with energy-efficient CFLs. I know you have heard all of this before. But you sort of filed it away under "someday I really should." That day is here. I bet you can reduce what you spend on your family's needs by 10% to 20% if you put your heart into it.

Insure Big Savings

Health insurance, car insurance, and home insurance (including renter's insurance) are three of the most important "needs" for every family. Without question, they are necessary expenses. But there are great ways to lower your insurance premiums. You are not to reduce your level of coverage, but rather, make sure you have taken advantage of every deal and discount possible.

- Raise your deductibles on all your policies. You can save 10% or more if you agree to a deductible of $500 or $1,000 rather than just $250. There's no need to keep a low deductible when you have a solid emergency savings fund that can cover any out-of-pocket expenses.
- Keep your auto and homeowner's/renter policies with one insurance company. You will be eligible for a 10–20% "multiline" discount.
- Designate one car as your "low mileage" car; if you keep annual mileage below 7,500–10,000 miles, the premium discount can be 10% or so.

■ Keep your FICO credit score above 720. Some insurers base the premium rate you are offered on your credit score. The higher your score, the more likely you are to get the best terms on all your insurance.

SITUATION: Three years ago, you and your partner agreed you would be a stay-at-home mom, but your partner's commission-based salary has fallen along with the bad economy, so you are stuck putting some expenses on your credit card, knowing you will not be able to pay it off in full.

ACTION: Base your financial decisions on what you have today, not what you had in the past. If your family can no longer afford to live on one income, you must consider going back to work.

I say that with great understanding of how hard this will be for you to consider. But remember, your long-term financial security requires making the right and honest choices today. And what is right is not always the same as what is easy. Going back to work when you believe it is far more important to be a stay-at-home parent is an emotionally charged and difficult step to contemplate, but in these tough times, it just might be necessary.

You need to focus on what is best for your children. I believe very strongly that financial security is what's best for your children. And if you cannot honestly keep your family financially secure—by being out of credit card debt, having a hefty savings fund, and keeping your retirement savings on track—you are not doing what is best for them.

Start by considering whether you (or your partner) can take on part-time work to supplement what is coming in from the one income. That may be a way to make more without having to rely completely on child care. But if that doesn't close the gap, you must think about taking on a bigger job. If it needs to be full-time, it needs to be full-time. Maybe not forever, but for now. That is not a punishment. It is a powerful choice to take action to build financial security for your family.

SITUATION: You can't afford to pay private-school tuition and invest the maximum in your retirement accounts.

ACTION: It might be time to rethink whether public school is the better move for your entire family. Look, I know this is a huge issue, and I am not suggesting you make a decision in the next 15 minutes about whether you can continue to send your 10-year-old to private school. But I also think it is shortsighted to presume that this expense is untouchable. If you are shortchanging your retirement savings, or if your emergency fund is nonexistent, you really need to think through whether you are doing the best for your child. If your issue is that you do not think your local public schools provide the quality education you want for your children, I want you to take a deep breath and consider moving to a community with a strong public school system. As I said, this is not a quick or easy decision. But I encourage you to at least start giving this serious consideration. Will home values and property taxes be higher in a town with high-quality schools? Probably. But I seriously doubt it will cost you the $30,000 or more a year it can take to send two children to private school.

SITUATION: You lost your job and can no longer afford to make the payments on your family's second car, but you owe more on the loan than you can get at trade-in.

ACTION: Call up your lender and see if you can get the loan terms modified. Ideally, you don't want to extend the length of the loan (that will increase your total cost over the life of the loan), but push to see if you can get the interest rate reduced. That will lower your costs. Or perhaps the lender will agree to a temporary period of reduced payments.

SITUATION: You just want your car to be repossessed already—you're sick of trying to keep up with the payments.

ACTION: If you know you can't afford the car, hand the car back to the lender rather than waiting for repossession. By proactively contacting the lender and giving the car back, you will avoid paying fees charged for repossession. And more important, you will avoid the trauma of having your car towed away from your work or home. You change the dynamic by making an embarrassing act into an act of responsibility.

SITUATION: You turned the car back in—or it was repossessed—but you were told you still owed the lender money.

ACTION: You are responsible for the difference between what you still owed on the loan and what the lender can recoup by reselling the car. If you can't cover that payment, you did not live up to your financial obligation. Whether you turned in the car or it was formally repossessed, failure to pay the balance will stay on your credit report for seven years.

SITUATION: You want to borrow from your 401(k) to keep up with the car payments.

ACTION: Do not touch your retirement savings. If you need to keep the car or you want to avoid having a repossession on your credit report, you must find other income sources to make the payment. Go back and review the Household Cash

Flow worksheet at the beginning of this chapter. If you need more cash, find it from spending less. The absolute worst move you can make is to pull money out of your 401(k). As I explain in detail in "Action Plan: Retirement," it is never wise to touch your retirement savings. Lose your job and your 401(k) loan will need to be repaid within a few months. Where are you going to come up with that money? That is going to create a big tax bill. Most important, money you spend today is money you won't have in retirement. Please consider every other possible alternative before you ever raid your 401(k) or other retirement savings.

SITUATION: Your eldest child heads to college next year and you're feeling like this is the last chance to take a long family vacation, even though it probably means putting $4,000 on your credit card that you won't be able to pay off immediately.

ACTION: You will get no argument from me that family time is a high priority. As you may have heard me say, my mantra is "People First, Then Money, Then Things." But that doesn't translate to giving you carte blanche to spend whatever you want to create those memories. They are not priceless memories. If you need to run up credit card debt to finance the memories, they have a very steep cost: a 15% interest rate, on average.

This is not about what you and your family deserve. We all deserve vacations. What you and your family need is to be safe. An unpaid credit card balance is not safe. Not having an emergency savings fund is not safe. Same goes for no retirement savings. If you haven't taken care of those priorities, you can't afford to take an expensive vacation. Period. That doesn't mean you can't spend time with your family and create lasting memories. Take the vacation—just do it at home, or closer to home, this year.

SITUATION: Your daughter is getting married. You have all dreamed of a big wedding, but your investments took a big hit last year and the only way you can afford the wedding is to put it on your credit card. This is a once-in-a-lifetime event, so it's not like you can just say no.

ACTION: You can, and must, say no. It is absolutely unacceptable to take on any sort of debt to pay for a wedding. No exceptions. I don't care what anyone dreamed of.

Do you deep down, *honestly*, believe that what you spend is a reflection of your love for your daughter? Do you honestly believe that it is better to take on $20,000 in credit card debt to impress your friends, rather than use that $20,000 for retirement savings? Step back for a moment and put this decision to the Need vs. Want test. What you and your daughter *want* is a big expensive wedding. But all that is really *needed* is an affordable wedding that is full of love.

SITUATION: You love giving gifts. It is important to you and something your friends and family have come to expect from you. You can't imagine stopping your gift-giving ways just to have more to save for yourself.

ACTION: As wonderful as it is that you give gifts, you and I both know that your friends and family don't love you because of the gifts. If you have yet to build an emergency savings fund that can cover eight months of living costs, you must curtail your gift giving so you can give yourself something far more important: security.

Besides, you are never, ever to buy gifts that you can't afford to pay for immediately. As I explained in "Action Plan: Credit," an unpaid credit card balance puts you at great risk of falling into a costly vicious cycle you will find it hard to climb out of. Worried what your friends and family will think if they don't receive an expensive gift this year? Come on. Do you really think anyone who cares about you would feel good if they received a gift with an unspoken price tag that said, *This gift cost $50 that I couldn't afford and means I will not be able to pay off my credit card bill this month?*

SITUATION: You are struggling to make ends meet, but you don't want to stop contributing to the charities you have supported in the past.

ACTION: Can you give time rather than money this year? I understand how important it is to help those in need. But you have important needs this year too. And it is not selfish to make your financial safety and security a priority. If you need to reduce or suspend your contributions this year to shore up your finances, that's the right and honest move for you to make.

I realize how hard this is, especially when charities are also feeling the pinch and are stepping up their requests for donations. But you must give only what you can honestly afford. If that means no financial contributions, that is okay. I encourage you to donate your time—or more of your time than you already give—to the causes you support. That is a valuable contribution. And to be honest, I think it can also have a great unintended benefit for you: It can be calming and rewarding to focus on what you can do through your actions to make the world a better place.

Now, that said, I also know how upsetting it can be to curtail helping others in need. Take another hard look at the Household Cash Flow worksheet and see if there are any costs you could pare back to free up a little money to contribute to the causes most important to you. Challenge yourself: "I want to cut $X a month in savings so I can continue to make charitable contributions this year." Often, having a specific goal makes it easier to focus on "wants" that you can do without.

SITUATION: Your son graduates from college in a few months and needs a car for work. He has asked you to cosign for a car loan.

ACTION: If you cannot cover the payments yourself, then you are never to cosign a loan. You need to understand that cosigning makes you legally responsible for the loan; in the event your child can't make the payment, you are expected to come up with the payment. Failure to do so will hurt your FICO score, not just your child's.

And let me define what it means to be able to afford to cosign: You have no credit card debt yourself. You are not struggling to make your mortgage and car payments. Even if you can afford to cover the payments, I want you to carefully consider what you are doing. If your child can't get a car loan on his own, you need to ask yourself why. Is he buying an expensive car when his budget can afford only a moderate-priced car? Is he focusing only on new cars for their "wow" factor, rather than buying a safe, reliable older car that is more affordable? Is there something the lender knows about his credit score that you don't—such as the fact that he is already up to his ears in credit card debt? Helping a child who is just getting started is fine, but helping a child who has already abused credit and has no clue how to be financially responsible is not acceptable.

If you decide to go ahead and cosign, I recommend that you be in charge of making the payment. I have seen too many parents cosign and assume their kid is making the payments, only to get a disturbing letter from the lender that the loan is delinquent and everyone's FICO score has been hurt. I know you are focused on your kid being an independent adult, but if he or she needs your help with a loan, you have every right to oversee the payment.

SITUATION: You need a new car, but you don't want to overreach and end up like your neighbor who had her car repossessed last year.

ACTION: Find out what you can afford with a maximum loan term of three years. That's what you can afford. It makes no financial sense to stretch into a more expensive car if you need to extend the loan term to four or five years. That's a colossal waste of money. What you need to understand is that a car is a lousy investment. It is guaranteed to lose money; the trade-in value will never cover the purchase price or the interest payments on a loan. Therefore, you want to keep your cost as low as possible by limiting yourself to a three-year loan. At www.bankrate.com, you can see what typical car rates are in your area and use the free calculator to figure out your monthly costs.

And I want to be clear, I am talking about a regular loan. No leases. Not now, not ever. With a car loan, you will eventually own the car free and clear and can drive it for five to seven more years without having to worry about your monthly payment. If you lease, you typically fall into a trap where you just keep rolling over into a new lease every three years. So you are always making payments. Given that we just discussed what a lousy investment a car is, why would you ever choose a never-ending cycle of car payments?

Before you start shopping, make sure your FICO credit score is at least 720. There are indeed great deals to be had, but you need to have a high credit score to get a loan with a reasonable rate. In a slowing economy, where lenders are downright scared to lend, they are going to offer reasonable deals only to borrowers with sparkling credit. In November 2009, a FICO score of 720 or better would make you eligible for a 6% car loan rate. If your score was 620–660, the rate was 13.4%.

I also recommend taking a look at certified preowned cars; these are used cars that come with a limited warranty. Make sure the warranty is from the manufacturer, not the dealership. Given the huge inventory of repossessed cars, you may be able to find an especially good deal on a used car. Sure, right now you might also be able to score a great deal on a new car if you have a solid FICO score. But please remember that the goal is to spend the least amount of money for a car that is safe and meets your commuting needs.

6

ACTION PLAN

Real Estate

New Rules for New Times

The fallout continues to course through every neighborhood. Foreclosures and short sales are not only restricted to the markets that saw the craziest gains from the bubble. Stable markets are being smacked hard, too, as spooked lenders impose new rules that make it much harder to qualify for a new mortgage, refinance an existing loan, or simply hold on to a once-sure thing, a home equity line of credit.

I hope you're not banking on a quick turnaround. There's actually a backlog of more bad news heading to market. According to First American CoreLogic, $170 billion of interest-only mortgages are scheduled to "reset" between mid-2009 and mid-2011. Another $400 billion will reset after that. Many of those homeowners face sharply higher monthly payments when their reset occurs, and refinancing their way out of trouble is unlikely given the erosion in home equity. The S&P/Case-Shiller index of home values in 20 large metro areas shed 30% between its 2006 peak and the summer of 2009.

The federal Making Home Affordable mortgage rescue plan launched in the spring of 2009 to help stabilize the markets has been a big disappointment. So far lenders have been slow to extend mortgage modifications and refinancing options to steady the market. Why is that? Well, one factor may be that a recent study by the Federal Reserve of Boston concluded that 40–50% of modified loans end up delinquent again within six months. Those are very sobering statistics for all of us, but particularly for lenders.

While the short-term outlook is anything but rosy, I do have something positive to say: I am still a big believer in homeownership. With one humongous caveat: Homeownership only makes sense if it is based on rational assumptions, not bubble-fueled dreams. That's what I said before the bubble, it's what I said during the bubble, and it's what I have to tell you now. The New Rules for Real Estate are nothing new if you've been listening to me all along; they're the rules and principles that were in place before the madness began.

Then: No-documentation, no-down-payment

adjustable-rate mortgages with artificially low initial payments offered like candy and taken on the assumption that fast and fat home-value appreciation would allow refinancing before the costly reset arrived.

Now: An application process that makes an Ivy League admissions process look like a cakewalk. Lenders sifting through reams of documentation of your financial life. Loan values based on what you can actually afford today with a 30-year fixed-rate mortgage instead of an exotic mortgage that requires a cascade of optimistic outcomes to work out okay for the lender and borrower (and not become the headache of the taxpayer).

Then: A land grab not seen since Manifest Destiny. Renters determined to get their piece of the American dream, owners giddily parlaying their equity riches into bigger and better McMansions or outsized lifestyles charged to their HELOCs. And all of it fueled, financed, and blessed by Wall Street and Washington.

Now: The steep decline in housing values lays bare another old-school truism: A home is not an insta-ATM or a four-sided retirement fund. Nor is there any financial magic that can transform pools of mortgages into risk-free investments.

But I am not about to write the obituary for homeownership. It is absolutely true that those of you who bought at the height of the craziness will not soon—if ever—see your home's value fully rebound. Those prices were artificially and irrationally inflated. There is no argument for a rebound all the way back to what was never real.

But let's also apply some perspective. The same index of home values that has declined 30% since the 2006 bubble peak is nonetheless nearly 20% higher than in January 2000. That return slightly lags inflation, but is far from a death knell. Add in the value derived from the use of leverage (you pay only a fraction of the purchase price from your personal savings and borrow the remainder) and the mortgage interest tax deduction, and it's clear there is still a strong argument for homeownership over the long term. Catch that last part? *Long term.* If you haven't already, drop the flipping dreams right now.

The New Rules for Real Estate require resetting expectations. Understand what your home is (shelter) and isn't (a liquid investment that banks 10–20% annual appreciation). Recognize that the financial community has hit the reset button and is once again insisting you pass a thorough vetting before qualifying for a mortgage.

For many of you, moving forward in today's real estate reality will require moving out. That is not easy to contemplate, I know. But if you cannot afford your mortgage, if you have been unable to renegotiate with your lender, if Washington and the banking industry do not arrive at a more effective process for extending assistance, then you will have no other choice. You start over by first letting go of what you can no longer control. A home should never be a source of stress. It should never be an overreach. If that's where you are at, it's time to make your move.

What you must do

- Push for a mortgage modification or refinance if your current loan is too expensive.
- Do not use credit cards or retirement funds to pay for a too-expensive home.
- Build a real savings fund; a HELOC should not be your safety net.
- Focus on your home's long-term value, not its price change from month to month.

Your Real Estate Action Plan

SITUATION: You can't afford the cost of your adjustable rate mortgage (ARM) since it reset, but you don't know what your options are.

ACTION: Start by contacting your lender and asking if there is any chance you can renegotiate (modify) your mortgage so your payments are more affordable. Please do this as soon as you think you're in trouble—over half of those whose homes are foreclosed never speak to their lender prior to foreclosure, according to the National Foundation for

Consumer Credit Counseling (NFCC). When you call, right away ask for a loan-mitigation or workout specialist. Be prepared to document your financial hardship as well as your ability to afford the modified loan. You can get advice about how to talk to your lender at www.hud.gov. Click on "Tips for Avoiding Foreclosure." Better yet, the NFCC has HUD-approved housing counselors who can advise you and will act as an advocate with your lender for the best resolution for your situation. Call 866-687-6322—you'll be automatically connected to the agency closest to you—or visit their Homeowner Crisis Resource Center at www .housinghelpnow.org.

SITUATION: You have heard there is a federal program to help qualified homeowners who are struggling to keep up with their mortgage payments, but you don't know what the program is, or whether you qualify.

ACTION: In February 2009 the Treasury Department announced a mortgage assistance program called Home Affordable. The program is two-pronged. The Home Affordable Refinance Program (HARP) is designed to help borrowers reduce their mortgage payments by getting a lower-cost loan. Your current mortgage can be as much as 125% of the current value of your home— meaning you are 25% underwater—and you may still qualify for the Home Affordable Refinance Program. I'll give more details below.

If you are unable to qualify for the Refinance Program you may be a candidate for the Home Affordable Modification Program (HAMP), in which your lender has a few different ways to push your payments down so you can afford to stay in your home.

Home Affordable is only intended for loans that were securitized or backed by Fannie Mae or Freddie Mac, though the intention is that lenders will offer this level of assistance to borrowers with other types of mortgages.

To learn more about Home Affordable, go to www.makinghomeaffordable.gov. This official website has tools to help you figure out your eligibility for both the refinance and modification programs. There is also a clear FAQ section that walks you through the ins and outs of the program.

As I write this in the fall of 2009, the programs have been slow to gain traction. Painfully slow. Lenders insist this is because it takes time to get their systems updated and personnel trained. Despite the slow start, the Treasury Department says Home Affordable is on pace to fulfill its initial goals: to help modify up to four million mortgages between 2009 and 2012 and help up to five million homeowners refinance into lower-cost mortgages.

But one thing is clear: If you want help, you are

going to need to be your own best advocate. It will take patience and persistence to get someone to consider your case. I wish it were different, but as we saw throughout 2009, many lenders have not been aggressive in seeking to help troubled homeowners. You are going to need to push and push to have a shot at getting a deal done. I encourage you to study the rules and regs at the Home Affordable website. There are very clear FAQs that explain what you need to know. The fact is, many of the people working at the banks are not always fully up to speed on how the programs work or not as motivated as you'd like to help you find solutions. You've heard the saying that knowledge is power? Well, it is so true in this case. Don't rely on someone else's knowledge. Be informed. It could make the difference in being able to stay in your home.

SITUATION: You don't know if you have a Fannie Mae or a Freddie Mac mortgage.

ACTION: If you are having trouble getting your lender to confirm what type of mortgage you have, use the following government resources:

For Fannie Mae:
1-800-7FANNIE (8 A.M. to 8 P.M. EST)
www.fanniemae.com/homeaffordable

For Freddie Mac:
1-800-FREDDIE (8 A.M. to 8 P.M. EST)
www.freddiemac.com/avoidforeclosure

SITUATION: You don't want to lose your home, but you can't afford the mortgage since the payment adjusted to a much higher level.

ACTION: See if you can qualify for the Home Affordable Modification Program. The home must be your primary residence, and only "conforming" Fannie and Freddie mortgages (typically $417,000 or less, but up to $729,750 in qualified high-cost regions) are covered. While the Home Affordable Refinance Program is limited to borrowers who are no more than 25% underwater, the loan modification program does not have any limit on how deeply underwater you may be.

Now, that doesn't mean everyone who is way behind on payments will automatically qualify for help. You still need to be able to afford the payments.

Here are the basic qualifying rules for the loan modification program:

- Your loan must be less than $729,750.
- You must live in the property. (No investment properties are covered.)
- You must be ready and willing to fully document your income. (Your most recent tax return and at least two current pay stubs are required.)

- You must have taken out the original mortgage before January 1, 2009.
- You must sign an affidavit (the lender will provide) that states you have a financial hardship.
- The payment on your first mortgage (including principal, interest, taxes, insurance, and home-owner's association dues, if applicable) must exceed 31% of your current gross income.
- If your total household debt—including other loans, credit card balances, and alimony pay-ments—total more than 55% of your income, you must agree to sign up for financial counseling.

Then it's up to the lender to figure out if you are a good candidate for a loan modification. The basic idea with this program is that lenders will agree (egged on by financial incentives courtesy of the government) to reduce the interest rate on quali-fied loans to as low as 2% in an effort to reduce your payments so you can afford to stay in your home. The way it will work is that lenders will size up your monthly debt-to-income ratio (DTI). The lender has to agree to reduce your interest rate to a point where your DTI is no more than 38%. Then the government jumps into the picture and will agree to pay half of the cost of having the lender reduce the payment even further to get you down to a more manageable 31% DTI.

The low loan rate is good for five years. Then it

will gradually increase—by no more than one percentage point a year—to a permanent fixed-rate loan tied to today's prevailing rates. That's about 5.2% as of November 2009. I want to be clear: Your permanent rate isn't the prevailing rate five years from now. If you qualify for this loan modification, you will lock in a maximum permanent rate based on the current fixed rate: about 5.2% in the early fall of 2009. So you might see your rate pushed as low as 2% right away to help you, but five years from now, when the rate starts "adjusting," the max it will hit cannot exceed whatever the market rate is on the day you first qualified for the program.

If the rate reduction doesn't get you down to the target 31% DTI, the lender can consider extending your loan term to 40 years to lower the monthly cost you pay, and can also consider "principal forbearance" where it stops charging interest on a portion of your loan amount for a set period.

The Home Affordable Modification Program expires at the end of 2012.

SITUATION: Your friends had their mortgage modified and now their credit score has gone way down.

ACTION: Unfortunately this can be an unintended consequence of modifying your loan. Some banks in 2009 reported modified loans as "not paid in full" or "delinquent," and that will indeed cause a credit score to drop. Loans that are part of the federal modification program are now supposed to be flagged as modifications—not late or delinquent payments—to the credit bureaus. FICO has no immediate plans to incorporate modifications into its scoring system, but once it compiles more data it may change the way it factors modifications into its scoring algorithms. I think the best approach is to understand that if you do a modification, your credit score may drop—either because your lender reports it erroneously, or because FICO could change its scoring system in the future. If you are sure a modification will allow you to stay in the home, then that can be a worthwhile trade-off.

SITUATION: You own a rental property you can no longer handle the payments on. You want to use one of the federal programs to rework your mortgage.

ACTION: Rental properties do not qualify for the Making Home Affordable programs. To qualify for a refinance or loan modification, the property must be your principal residence.

SITUATION: Your mortgage is not owned or securitized by Fannie Mae or Freddie Mac, and you are worried that means you are not eligible for HAMP.

ACTION: Check with your lender. You may still be able to work out a deal using HAMP. While the program is mandatory for loans that are held or securitized by Fannie Mae and Freddie Mac, lenders can choose to use the program for other types of loans as well. In fact, HAMP offers financial incentives for lenders to participate. So don't give up if you find your mortgage is not held by Fannie or Freddie. Bug your lender as often and as persistently as needed to find out whether they will consider any mortgage workout with you.

SITUATION: You are still current with your mortgage payments, but they are stretching you so thin you worry you may not be able to keep up.

ACTION: See if you can qualify for the Home Affordable Refinance Program. When the program was first launched in the spring of 2009, it was limited to homeowners whose mortgage balance was no more than 105% of the current appraised value of their home. That rule was later extended to 125%. You can now be as much as 25% underwater and still qualify for HARP.

Here's what it takes to have a shot at the Home Affordable Refinance Program:

- The loan on your property is owned or guaranteed by Fannie Mae or Freddie Mac. (See details above for how to find out.)

- At the time you apply, you are current on your mortgage payments. The government's definition of "current" typically means that during the past year you have not been more than 30 days late.
- The amount you owe on your first lien mortgage does not exceed 125% of the current market value of your property.
- You have a reasonable ability to pay the new mortgage payments.
- The refinance improves the long-term affordability or stability of your loan.

HARP is currently scheduled to expire on June 10, 2010. You must have the new refinanced mortgage in place by that date. Please check my website for an update on whether this deadline is extended past June 10, 2010.

SITUATION: You have a second mortgage or HELOC but you were told you do not qualify for HARP.

ACTION: You may still qualify, but it is up to the lender that owns your second mortgage or HELOC to agree to the refinance. If there is any way you can pay off the second mortgage/HELOC it may help you get your refinance approved.

SITUATION: Your mortgage is not owned or securitized by Fannie Mae or Freddie Mac.

ACTION: You may still be able to work out a deal with your lender. Though Home Affordable requires all Fannie and Freddie mortgages to be considered, lenders can choose to use the same programs for other mortgages too. To be honest, not all lenders have been eager to help, but some have. As I said earlier, you can't wait for someone to call you up and offer assistance. You need to be aggressive in asking for help and pushing your case forward.

SITUATION: Your mortgage has become too expensive, but you don't want to lose your home and upset your family.

ACTION: If you can't negotiate a lower payment with your lender and none of the programs mentioned above can help you, then I am so sorry to tell you that you must try to sell your home—and the sooner the better. I know it is excruciatingly painful to consider, but it is also a simple decision. You cannot stay in a home you cannot afford. Remember, the right moves are honest moves.

SITUATION: You're thinking that if you can just hold on to your home for another year, the market will recover and you will be able to refinance your mortgage.

ACTION: Do not base your decisions today on the magical hope that somehow everything will work out if you can just wait for the big rebound.

If the only way you can hang on depends on a fast and dramatic rebound, your honest move is to try and sell your home.

SITUATION: When you bought your home three years ago, the lender steered you into an ARM and said that you would be able to refinance before the first rate adjustment. But now you're being told you can't refinance because you have no equity in the home.

ACTION: Make sure to check in with the lender to see if you can qualify for the Home Affordable Refinance Program (go to www.makinghome affordable.gov to learn more). If you are turned down and you will not be able to afford the mortgage when your interest rate resets, then I am afraid the best thing to do would be to try to sell your home.

SITUATION: To eke by and make the mortgage payment, you have resorted to using your credit card to cover more expenses. You credit card balance is now ballooning out of control.

ACTION: Again, push to see if your mortgage can be modified. If not, you must consider selling, because using your credit card is not a good solution to this difficult problem. You need to look a few months into the future and realize that before you know it you will have reached your card's credit limit. Then what? You will have a ton of credit card debt and a mortgage you still can't afford. All you have done is delay the inevitable, and in the process you have added thousands of dollars in credit card debt.

For those of you who are stubborn and want to use your credit cards to help you stay in your house, I need you to review what I explained in "Action Plan: Credit." I have never advocated piling on credit card debt, but in the wake of the financial crisis that began in 2008, it is doubly dangerous. As I write this in the fall of 2009, credit card companies are especially wary of anyone who seems to be heading for trouble; a rising unpaid balance will set off warning bells at the credit card company. It can result in your credit limit being cut, your account being shut down (you won't be able to make new charges, but you will still be responsible for your existing balance), and your interest rate could skyrocket. Please don't compound your mortgage problem with a credit card problem.

I know this is hard to consider, but if you really can't afford the mortgage today, it is better to move than to go deeper into debt trying to hold on. Of course, I am assuming you have done absolutely everything possible to come up with the money to pay the mortgage. In "Action Plan: Spending," I have suggestions about how to cut your expenses so you have more money left to pay the mortgage or address other financial goals.

SITUATION: You want to make a withdrawal from your 401(k) and use the money to help you keep current with your mortgage payments.

ACTION: Don't do it. If you use up your retirement money today, what will you live on in retirement?

I see so many people making this huge mistake these days. I understand the thinking: You are desperate to hang on to your house and will do anything not to fall into foreclosure. So you empty out your 401(k), paying income tax on the withdrawal and may also be hit with a 10% penalty for money taken out before you are 59½. But then, six months later, you find yourself back in the same hole: You have used up all the money you withdrew from your 401(k) and you are once again falling behind on your mortgage. So all you have done is delay the inevitable: that you can't really afford this mortgage. But in the process you have wiped out any retirement savings. For nothing.

It's also important to know that money you have in a 401(k) or IRA is protected if you ever have to file bankruptcy. You get to keep that money no matter what. This isn't a pleasant scenario to ponder, but let's think about what happens in a really dire situation: You have $20,000 in your 401(k) that you withdraw. After tax and the 10% penalty, you are left with about $15,000. That helps pay the bills for another few months, but once you have used it up, you are back where you started: You can't afford the home. So you lose the home. And now you have no retirement savings.

If instead you kept the $15,000 invested for another 10 years and it earned even a conservative 5% return, you would have nearly $25,000 saved up. And that money will never be taken away in a bankruptcy.

SITUATION: You want to take a loan from your 401(k) and use the money to help you keep current with your mortgage payments.

ACTION: A loan is no better than a withdrawal in this situation. Don't do it. You probably know I am not a big fan of this move. Taking out a loan means you end up being taxed twice on the money you withdraw. And there's the risk that if you are laid off you typically must pay back the loan within a few months. So if you take out the loan, get laid off, and can't pay it back ASAP, you will run into another tax problem: The loan is treated as a withdrawal and you are stuck paying the 10% early-withdrawal penalty (if you are under 59½) as well as income tax.

SITUATION: You can't afford your mortgage payments, but what you owe on your mortgage is more than the house will sell for.

ACTION: Push your lender to agree to a short sale.

In a short sale, the lender accepts whatever you can sell your house for in today's market, even if that is less than the outstanding balance on your mortgage. The lender is agreeing that once you hand over all proceeds from the sale, your mortgage will be considered settled; any shortfall between the sale price and your balance will be forgiven.

Lenders may be open to this arrangement if they believe what they can get from the short sale is more than the cost they will incur if they foreclose on your home. That said, it is by no means easy to get lenders to agree to a short sale. But it is worth asking. The impact on your FICO credit score is no different from what it would be if you went through foreclosure (see details below), but it is a less traumatic way to walk away.

SITUATION: You are worried a short sale will hurt your FICO score.

ACTION: It will, but it is better to be honest now than hang on and make your financial life (and credit score) even worse by trying to stay in an un-affordable home.

The mortgage you took out was a legal contract in which you agreed to repay the amount you borrowed (the principal) plus interest. In a short sale, you are allowed to repay less than the amount you borrowed. You did not live up to your end of the contract, and that is going to hurt your FICO score. A short sale will stay on your credit report for seven years (though you won't see the term "short sale" on your credit report; lenders use different terms, sometimes describing short sales as "settled"), the same as a foreclosure. The impact of a short sale (and foreclosure) on your FICO score lessens as time goes by.

If you anticipate you will go through a short sale, it becomes extra important to keep your credit card balances paid off. I know this is difficult, given the fact that you are dealing with serious financial issues, but you need to make this a priority, because once your FICO score drops because of the short sale, your credit card company may get nervous and that typically leads to raising your interest rate. And the last thing you can afford is a credit card balance with a 32% interest rate. Please note that this tax break is only for a short sale of a principal residence. If you use a short sale to get out from under a losing rental property, you can indeed be hit with the tax.

SITUATION: You have heard that if you agree to a short sale you will have a big tax bill from the IRS, and you don't have the money to pay for that.

ACTION: Relax. You will not owe income tax on the amount of the debt that is forgiven, as long as the short sale occurs before 2012. Up to $2 million in forgiven debt is shielded from income tax for married couples filing a joint tax return ($1 million for individuals).

SITUATION: You were turned down for a short sale. Is foreclosure your only option?

ACTION: Probably. Your only other option is a "deed in lieu of foreclosure," where you hand over the deed to your home to the lender, who then takes the house without going through the formal foreclosure process. While this is an option, it is not widely offered by lenders. Short sale or foreclosure is a more likely alternative.

SITUATION: Will you have to move out immediately when the bank starts the foreclosure process?

ACTION: Foreclosure law varies by state. Lenders will typically start the foreclosure process once you are three months behind in payments.

In about half the states, foreclosures must go through the court system; the other half use procedures that don't require judicial action. For example, some states allow for what is known as a "power of sale," in which mortgage companies—or whoever is empowered under the mortgage document—can handle the foreclosure process. In either type of foreclosure, you will receive notification from the foreclosing party that the foreclosure process has started; typically you will have from a few weeks to a few months (depending on your state's laws) to reinstate the loan by paying up what you owe. (For a roundup of state foreclosure statutes, see Stephen Elias's *Foreclosure Survival Guide,* Nolo Press, 2008; updates to the list will be published in the legal updates area on nolo.com.)

If you do not get current on your mortgage in the allotted time, the foreclosure proceeds, and your home is sold or the lender takes possession. Though you have the right to remain in your home until you are ordered out by a court after the foreclosure sale, many lenders encourage foreclosed owners to leave by making a "cash for keys" offer, money paid for your leaving voluntarily instead of requiring the new owner to obtain a court eviction order. A good overview of the foreclosure process is at www.credit.com/life_stages/overcoming/Understanding-Foreclosure.jsp.

SITUATION: You've been contacted by a foreclosure "rescue specialist" who promises to help you avoid foreclosure for a fee.

ACTION: Don't fall for this. Legitimate foreclosure consultants do not seek you out; you go to them. The huge number of at-risk borrowers has created a whole new opportunity for scam artists who can easily find victims by scouting public records for notices of default. The most common ploy: They'll offer to negotiate a deal with your lender if you pay the fee first; once you pay, they're gone. An even nastier scam involves getting you to sign documents for a new loan that will supposedly make your existing mortgage current, but instead you've been tricked into surrendering the title to the scammer in exchange for a "rescue" loan.

If you're facing foreclosure, get help you can trust. Start with the National Foundation for Consumer Credit Counseling, which will put you in touch with a housing counselor in your area: call 866-687-6322. More information on foreclosure scams is available at their Homeowner Crisis Resource Center, housinghelpnow.org, and at the FTC site, www.ftc.gov/bcp/edu/pubs/consumer/credit/cre42.shtm. If you think you've been a victim of foreclosure fraud, contact the Federal Trade Commission at ftc.gov or call 1-877-FTC-HELP, or your state attorney general's office.

SITUATION: You are worried that going through a foreclosure means you will never be able to buy another house.

ACTION: You will be eligible to buy a house in the future if you take steps today to start rebuilding your FICO score. There is no sugarcoating this: A foreclosure, as well as a short sale, will be a big negative mark on your FICO credit score. But it is not a permanent stain. The foreclosure stays on your credit report for seven years; each year its impact on your FICO credit score lessens. This is no different from a short sale.

Because you will likely see your FICO score drop, you want to do your best to reduce any unpaid credit card balances if you anticipate going through foreclosure. I know this is going to be hard to pull off, given that you are obviously dealing with some serious financial challenges. But please do your best to keep your credit card balances low. When your FICO score goes down, your credit card company may become nervous that you are in trouble. That might result in the card company's lowering your credit line. And as we discussed in "Action Plan: Credit," that starts a vicious cycle that can lead to a huge increase in your interest rate.

SITUATION: With real estate prices lower, you are wondering if it's a good time to buy a home.

ACTION: I still believe that over time a home can be one of the most satisfying investments you can make, but you have to make sure you can afford it. By "afford it" I mean not just being able to meet the monthly mortgage payments and expenses, but you have to be able to make those payments for at least eight months if you don't have income coming in. Why eight months? Because if by chance you were to lose your job, it could take many months to find a new one. I certainly hope you would find a great new job quickly, but if we find ourselves in a deep, slow recession, it could take longer to find a job than you anticipate. I want you to be in a position to know you have savings set aside to cover the mortgage while you job-hunt.

As for timing: I recommend buying only if you intend to stay put for at least five years, preferably longer. I don't care what sort of deal you think you can get, it makes no sense to buy a home today if you suspect you might move in a few years. If you buy today, prices may not go up much over the next few years; in fact, in some areas they could still go down. And it's important to remember that when you go to sell you will be responsible for paying an agent a sales commission of 5–6%. That could wipe out any appreciation you might see over the next year or two . . . or five, depending on where you live.

And don't even think about buying if you have yet to save up at least 10% of the purchase price for a down payment. Did I say 10%? I should add that 20% is even better. Though there are some government programs that require smaller down payments, the new reality is that the only way many homeowners will qualify for a regular mortgage is if they can make a solid down payment.

The last requirement I have for potential buyers is that you can buy your home with a standard 30-year, fixed-rate mortgage. Instead of "betting" on an adjustable-rate loan, or that you will have enough equity in three or five years to refinance, I think it is smarter to stick with a 30-year fixed-rate so you never have to worry about your payment rising.

SITUATION: You want to take advantage of the low real estate prices in your area, but there's no way you can afford a 10% down payment.

ACTION: The days of no-down-payment loans are gone, and with any luck they will never return. You have to realize that if the millions of homeowners who bought a house with no down payment during the housing boom had been required to make a down payment, we would not be in this mess right now. Without the down payment, those people would not have been allowed to buy in the first place.

And I have always said that if you can't afford to make a down payment, it's a sign you can't afford a home.

As of November 2009 many lenders typically insist you make at least a 10% down payment, and in some markets you may need a 20% down payment. You can secure a low down payment option if you qualify for an FHA-insured loan. The Federal Housing Administration loan program allows home purchases with down payments as low as 3.5%. And you can use gifts from friends and family to fulfill the down payment requirement. But please remember what I said: Being able to use some of your own savings for a down payment is an important signal to yourself that you are ready to own. It is a sign of commitment and responsibility. If you can't put anything toward the down payment, I think that's a good indication that you should slow down and save up for a year or two.

In the past the FHA mortgage program had low loan limits that made them impractical for many buyers. But for 2010 the limits are as much as $729,750 in some high-cost areas. You can ask an FHA-approved lender what the current limit is in your region, or check the FHA's website at https://entp.hud.gov/idapp/html/hicostlook .cfm.

SITUATION: Your friends bought their first home in 2009 and got an $8,000 tax credit. You don't know if you can qualify for a similar tax break this year.

ACTION: The $8,000 First Time Home Buyer Tax Credit has been extended through April 30, 2010. To claim the credit you must be in contract by the end of April and the deal must close by June 30, 2010. Individuals with income below $150,000 and married couples with joint income below $225,000 are eligible for the credit. The home you purchase must be your primary residence and the purchase price must be below $800,000.

Members of the military who are deployed for at least 90 days outside the United States have until June 30, 2011, to claim the credit.

SITUATION: You don't know what purchase price you can afford for a house.

ACTION: First-time buyers must understand that paying $1,000 in monthly rent does not mean you can afford a mortgage of $1,000 a month. In addition to the base mortgage, you will also have to pay property tax, home insurance, and, if your down payment is less than 20%, private mortgage insurance. You also have to be ready to pay for repairs and maintenance costs—you're the landlord now! If you add up all those other non-mortgage costs, your monthly bill can be 30% to 40% more than the basic mortgage. So if you were to take on a $1,000 mortgage, your monthly housing costs could actually be closer to $1,300–$1,400 a month. Yes, it is true that you will get a tax break as a homeowner; the interest on your mortgage payments is tax deductible. That's a help, but not a solution.

The best way to figure out how much you can afford is to use an online calculator (go to www .bankrate.com) to figure out the base mortgage amount. Then add at least 30% to that amount and ask yourself if you can honestly handle that cost. If not, look to buy a less expensive home. The goal is to afford a home comfortably, not to stretch and gamble.

SITUATION: You would like to sell your home and downsize to a smaller home, but after paying the broker's fee, you worry that you won't have enough money for a down payment on your next home.

ACTION: Through April 30, 2010, if you sell a home and then purchase another primary residence you may be able to collect a $6,500 federal tax credit.

The eligibility rules are the same as with the First Time Homebuyer Credit explained above:

To claim the credit you must be in contract by the end of April, and the deal must close by June 30, 2010. Individuals with income below $150,000 and married couples with joint income below $225,000 are eligible for the credit. The home you purchase must be your primary residence and the purchase price must be below $800,000.

Members of the military who are deployed for at least 90 days outside the United States have until June 30, 2011, to claim the credit.

SITUATION: You bought your house 10 years ago and have a lot of equity, but you wonder if you should sell now and just rent.

ACTION: Your home is not a stock that you buy and sell based on its short-term value. If you enjoy your home, if you can afford your home, and if you don't need to sell right now, stay put.

Assuming you don't have to move, why move? Especially when you consider that you'll have to pay the 6% sales commission along with the cost and hassle of the actual move.

SITUATION: Two years ago, you took out a HELOC that you never used but kept in case you ran into an emergency. Your lender just told you it was revoking your HELOC.

ACTION: You must have a regular savings account funded with your own cash. You cannot rely on either a HELOC or credit card line of credit to be available in an emergency. When the economy hits a hard stretch, lenders get scared and look for ways to reduce their risk. That's exactly what happened in 2008 and 2009; as home values fell, lenders reduced or revoked HELOCs. With less equity in your home, you suddenly look a lot riskier to your HELOC lender.

SITUATION: You have an open HELOC and are wondering if you should tap it now and put the money into a savings account to serve as your emergency savings fund.

ACTION: Fund a savings account from real savings, not by increasing your debt. It is absurd to take on more debt. Don't tell me you will just use your savings to cover the HELOC payment if you get laid off. Wake up. You will need that money to pay your basic living costs, so why would you want to add to that monthly nut?

If you want to build a real, honest savings account, check out my advice in "Action Plan: Spending," for ways to find money to put toward your most important goals.

SITUATION: You planned on using a HELOC to help pay for your child's college costs, but your home lost so much value, you doubt you will be able to pay for school with a HELOC.

ACTION: Be grateful market forces didn't lure you into this bad move. I have never liked it when families increase their housing debt to pay for school. It typically leaves parents severely in debt just at the point when they should be focusing on paying off their mortgage debt, not increasing it, to prepare for retirement.

Don't worry, you have solid loan options to cover college costs. Please check out "Action Plan: Paying for College."

SITUATION: You were counting on booming home prices to help pay for your retirement.

ACTION: Time to get serious about saving money from your paycheck. As I stated earlier in this chapter, I am still a big believer that your home is a solid long-term investment. But that means it will, on average, rise in value at a pace that is only one percentage point or so ahead of inflation. That's not going to fill your retirement nest egg.

If you are over 50, make it your goal to take advantage of the extra "catch-up" amounts you are allowed to invest in your 401(k) and IRA. In 2010, you can invest an extra $5,500 in your 401(k) if you are over 50, for a total maximum contribution of $22,000. You can also contribute an extra $1,000 to your IRA in 2010, for a total of $6,000.

Can't imagine where to come up with extra cash? Make sure you read "Action Plan: Spending."

SITUATION: You can afford your home, but you worry that you have made a lousy investment.

ACTION: Love your home for what it is. Yes, it is an investment, but not one whose value you should be charting on a monthly or annual basis. If you can afford your home today, the best thing you can do is not worry about the current turmoil in the housing market.

Homes remain a solid long-term investment. But let's review what I mean by solid. The long-term trend—and I am talking decades, not a few years—is that homes on average rise in value at a pace that is about one percentage point better than inflation. One way to look at the massive bursting of the real estate bubble that began in 2007 is that it is in fact a painful correction that brings things back to a level based on a more moderate rate of appreciation.

In the meantime, your home is where you live. It is a refuge, a place where you and your family build memories. It is also a fine tax break.

SITUATION: You are near retirement age and planned on paying off your mortgage ahead of schedule. You're not sure that still makes sense.

ACTION: If you are in a home you plan to live in forever, accelerating your mortgage payments still makes terrific sense. Owning your home free and clear will provide a tremendous sense of financial security in retirement. The only caveat: If you have credit card debt to pay off, make that your priority before you focus on extra mortgage payments. And always make sure you invest enough in your 401(k) to receive the company match.

If you have all that taken care of, then paying down your mortgage is a smart move. I have always been a proponent of getting rid of mortgage debt before you retire. The best way to ensure that you will be able to afford your home in retirement is to know you own it free and clear and have to use retirement funds only for property tax and maintenance costs.

If you own your home free and clear, you also have the option of borrowing money through a reverse mortgage if you find you need extra income in retirement.

One important note: You are not to use money set aside in your emergency savings fund to pay off your mortgage. Emergency cash is for an *emergency*. Don't raid the savings to pay off the mortgage, or for any other goal for that matter.

SITUATION: You rent a home and have always paid your landlord on time, but you just found out you have to move out because the landlord did not pay the mortgage and the bank is foreclosing on the home.

ACTION: A federal law passed in May 2009 provides important protection for renters of foreclosed properties. Unless the new owner of the property intends to live in the home, the renter must be allowed to stay in the property through the end of the lease. And even if the renter is to be evicted, there must be 90 days' advance notice given. This federal law will remain in effect through 2012. If your state or municipality has regulations in place that offer more protections for renters, those rules will apply.

SITUATION: You are in good shape financially, with enough money to put down 20%. You wonder if now is the right time to get a good deal on a vacation home so you can rent it out and make some money.

ACTION: Be very careful here. Many of you looking to buy vacation homes or investment real estate may not be looking at the big picture, and that could get you in trouble. If you need to rent out this property in order to make the mortgage payments, then I would say do not touch this "opportunity" with a 10-foot pole. Why? Because if something happens and your tenants cannot pay the rent, how are you going to pay the mortgage? You need to know that you can afford the payments month in and month out, regardless of rental income. Remember, too, that during periods of economic turmoil, more vacation-home owners are apt to want to rent out their properties, and that's bad for you. More competition, that is, for fewer potential renters.

And at the risk of repeating myself, let me say yet again: If you have one penny of credit card debt, if you do not have retirement savings, if you do not have an emergency savings fund that can cover your living costs for at least eight months, if you are still paying off your primary mortgage or have an outstanding HELOC balance, you cannot afford a vacation home. Denied!

7

Paying for College

New Rules for New Times

In the wake of the financial crisis, the already daunting task of financing your children's college education has shifted from hard to "are you kidding me?"

The value of 529 college savings plans was battered during the bear market, dropping more than 20% on average. The sad fact is that many families were caught holding way too much stock in their portfolios with their kids just a few years away from freshman orientation. More to the point, many families found out too late that the age-based target funds they had relied on to set the proper mix of stocks and bonds for them were in fact invested too aggressively for students just a year or two away from freshman year.

Meanwhile, you are rethinking your internal

financial calculus. With the dawning reality that you need to save a lot more for retirement—and soon—you lay awake at night wondering where the money for the 401(k) and IRA will come from. Even your backstop has disappeared; though I never advocated tapping home equity to pay for college, I know many of you thought of your home as your "in case of emergency" option if the savings and aid didn't cover what was needed. Now that option, too, is off the table for many of you.

And it's not likely schools will be able and willing to fill your financing void. We've all seen the headlines about the losses and lack of liquid investments affecting private college endowments. Public schools, too, have been reeling from state budgets cuts and massive revenue declines.

The New Rules for Saving for College dictate that tuition is a family project. You must recognize that retirement does indeed move to the front of the class in terms of where you direct your savings. You've no doubt heard me say this before: There are loans for college, but no loans for retirement. With less saved up for college, you and your child will need to study up on the smartest loans for school. As you contemplate the cost of those loans, it is necessary and honorable to sit down and talk through what school is the best fit. This is not just about choosing the best education and the perfect campus fit. Making sure you find an affordable financial fit is also important. You must think long and hard about how much debt you are comfortable taking on to send your kid to school.

Any amount, you say? You just flunked your first college finance quiz. If you borrow so much that you will be hard-pressed to make the payments and forced to cut corners on other goals, then you have to question your approach. A college degree is unequivocally smart. A college degree that leaves you and your child with bone-crushing debt is not acceptable. According to finaid.org, two-thirds of college students now graduate with debt, and the average amount owed is more than $23,000. This when the average salary for recent graduates fell 1.7% in 2009—that is, for the grads lucky enough to get a job.

I want to reiterate that I am not questioning the value of a college degree. I am asking that you and your children together become savvy shoppers. Quality of education matters. A campus that feels right matters. Just promise yourself you will make the cost factor part of the decision too.

What you must do

- If your child is heading to college within four years and your college savings are in the stock market, you should begin to phase it out of the market, so that you are 100% out by the time he or she is 17.
- Make federal Stafford loans your first option when loan shopping.

- If Stafford loans are not enough, parents should consider a PLUS loan. Significant changes to this program make this a viable option for many more families.
- Stay away from private student loans at all costs.
- If you are graduating from college with student loan debt, know your repayment options.

Your Action Plan: Paying for College

SITUATION: Your child is set to go to college next year. You want to stop putting money in your 401(k) and use those funds to pay for your child's education. Should you?

ACTION: No, no, no. Your retirement account must come first.

There is nothing—and I mean nothing—that takes precedence over locking in short-term security (in the form of an eight-month emergency savings account) and providing for long-term security by continuing to invest for your retirement.

I am not insensitive to the importance you place on providing the opportunity for your children to achieve and realize their greatest potential in life. And I am aware that it is not an easy thing to do to ask that your children share the cost of college by taking out student loans. But it is necessary. Please review "Action Plan: Retirement" for my advice on why it is never wise to stop or suspend saving for retirement, and why down markets can actually be a good thing if you are saving for a goal that is 10, 20, or 30 years away.

Most important to keep in mind is that you need your retirement money waiting for you in retirement. If it's not there, you could end up being a financial burden for your kids. If you fail to save today, what will you have to live on in retirement? Now, don't worry, I am not suggesting you leave your kids high and dry. As I explain in the following pages, both your child and you can take out federal loans to help pay for school.

SITUATION: You want to borrow from your 401(k) to cover the college bills.

ACTION: Don't you dare. It is never smart to touch your retirement savings to pay for another expense. Even if you have every intention of paying back the loan, there's simply no guarantee that you will be able to. And to repeat myself: What happens if you lose your job? You need to understand that any outstanding loan must be repaid within a few months or the loan is considered a withdrawal. That will trigger income tax on the entire amount you withdrew and typically a 10% early-withdrawal penalty if you are not 55 or older when you are laid off. If you need to come up with money for college, federal loans are the best option.

SITUATION: You want to use IRA savings to pay for your child's college tuition.

ACTION: As I said earlier, raiding your retirement funds to pay for college is not ideal. What will you live on in retirement? Another potential problem is that taking an early distribution from an IRA can affect your child's financial aid eligibility; the withdrawal will be treated as parental income, and that is a major factor in determining aid. My advice: Don't touch your IRA to pay for college.

For those of you who refuse to follow this advice, I do want to point out that if you withdraw money early from your IRA to pay for college costs you will not owe the 10% early-withdrawal penalty typically charged by the IRS on withdrawals made before age 59½. You may, however, owe income tax on the withdrawn money. Withdrawals of money you contributed to a Roth IRA will not be taxed, though earnings may be taxed. Money withdrawn from a traditional IRA may be subject to income tax.

SITUATION: You have no credit card debt and your retirement savings is on track, so you want to start a college savings fund, but you are not sure about the best way to invest.

ACTION: A 529 savings plan is one of the easiest and smartest ways to save for future college costs. Money you invest in a plan grows tax-deferred, and eventual withdrawals will be tax-free if they are used for "qualified" college costs. There is also no income-eligibility requirement; all families can set up a 529, and contributions can come from parents, grandparents, aunts, uncles, friends. In addition to 529 plans, there are indeed other savings options, such as Coverdell Educational Savings Accounts and U.S. savings bonds. I highly recommend you check out the website www .savingforcollege.com; it is hands-down the most informative site for parents who want to save for their kids' future college costs.

SITUATION: You have been putting money into a 529 plan every month since your little one was born. After living through the bear market that began in 2008, you're thinking you should move your money out of your plan's stock fund choice and into bonds or cash offered by the 529 plan. Good idea?

ACTION: Nooo. If you have at least 10 years until you need your money, you have time on your side to ride out volatility in the stock market. You don't want to stop investing in stocks, or pull out of stocks when you have time on your side; the smart move is to invest *more* in your 529 plan's stock fund, not less!

SITUATION: The bear market that began in 2008 spooked you, and now you want to quit the 529 and move all the money into a safe bank account.

ACTION: Do not do this, because it can have significant tax consequences. Money you leave in a 529 that is eventually used to pay for college expenses is free of federal tax and state income tax too (except in Alabama, should you use a non-Alabama 529). But if you pull the money out, you can be hit with a 10% penalty tax on any earnings on that account. Below you will find my recommendations for the right mix of stocks and bonds in your 529, based on your child's age. If you feel you simply can't stand to remain invested in stocks, then shift the money into a stable-value account within the 529.

SITUATION: Your child starts college in two years and your 529 is 100% in stocks.

ACTION: This is too risky. When your child is within a year or two of freshman year, you no longer have time on your side. You are going to have to start using that money sooner rather than later, so you need to make sure your money is safe and sound in the 529 plan's bond or money market fund. My recommendation is that you slowly shift money out of stocks and into bonds starting at age 14. You goal should be that you are completely out of stocks by the time your child is five years from *senior year in college*—typically, that is age 17.

Under age 14:	100% stocks
Age 14:	75% stocks
Age 15:	50% stocks
Age 16:	25% stocks
Age 17:	0% stocks

If your current allocation exceeds those targets, I recommend you rebalance your portfolio ASAP.

Those of you who have opted for a fund in your 529 plan that automatically changes its allocation as your child gets closer to college still need to pay attention and understand how much you will have invested in stocks when your child hits 14, 15, 16, 17, and 18. I have seen plans with up to 50% in stocks a year or two before the child will enter school. That's unacceptable.

If you find your target fund overloads on stocks close to college, I recommend moving out of the target option, finding the best low-cost stock and bond fund options offered by the plan, and putting your money in both those funds according to the strategy above.

SITUATION: You have time on your side, but after watching your child's college fund plummet, you just can't stomach keeping the entire portfolio invested in stocks.

ACTION: It's fine to move up to 20% into bonds. A small amount of bonds will reduce your portfolio's overall loss in a bear market, and if that helps you stay committed to investing and helps you sleep better, then it is the right move for you.

SITUATION: You tried to move money out of your 529 plan's stock fund and into the bond fund option, but you were told you had to wait until next year.

ACTION: Understand that an IRS rule requires 529 plans to limit participants to rebalancing their portfolio just once a year. The reasoning is that you can't be trusted to be a patient long-term investor, so this rule was meant to keep you from day-trading your kid's college fund. As if. A special regulation in effect in 2009 allowed two rebalancing moves during the year. Please check my website for an update on whether this rule was extended past 2009.

SITUATION: Your family doesn't qualify for financial aid (or the aid package isn't as much as you expected), but you don't have money to pay the college bills this year.

ACTION: First, you need to take a deep breath. I know it is stressful. I know it is upsetting. But you do have options. One of the great misconceptions is that federal loans are only for students and families that meet certain income-eligibility rules. That is absolutely incorrect. In addition to the many forms of aid and loans that are income-based, there are also affordable loans available for students and parents regardless of family wealth or income. If you find that your school's financial aid package is not enough to cover all your costs, you can supplement that aid with non-income-based loans.

The first step is for your child, the student, to apply for both subsidized and unsubsidized Stafford loans. Yes, your child borrows first, not you. Staffords are the cheapest loan options. If you want to make a side agreement with your child that you will help with the repayment of the Staffords, that's fine. But please get over any concern or guilt about having your child borrow first.

If you meet income-eligibility rules, your child may qualify for a subsidized Stafford loan. (It is typically part of a financial aid package you receive from the school.) Subsidized means the federal government pays the interest on the loan while your kid is in school. The interest rate for a subsidized loan is 5.6% for the 2009–2010 school year. Subsidized Staffords issued in the 2010–2011 school year will have a 4.5% interest rate. Loans issued for the 2011–2012 school year will carry a rock-bottom 3.4% interest rate. That's a fraction of what you can end up paying for a private student loan. But here's what so many people fail to understand: *Anyone, regardless of income, can apply for an unsubsidized Stafford.* The interest rate is fixed at 6.8% and interest payments are the responsibility of the student. (The rate on unsubsidized Staffords will not change for the 2010–2011 and 2011–2012 academic years.) The student can opt to not pay interest while in school and have it added to the loan balance. Here's a suggestion: If Grandma and Grandpa want to know how they can help with school, ask them to cover the unsubsidized Stafford interest payments so their grandchild can graduate with a lower loan balance. If that's not an option, your child can work during school and make the interest payments him- or herself.

SITUATION: How much can you borrow on a Stafford loan in 2009?

ACTION: For the 2009–2010 academic year, freshmen can now borrow $5,500; sophomores $6,500; and juniors and seniors $7,500. Children who are not claimed as dependents by their parents are eligible for higher amounts. For subsequent years you can check the finaid.org website.

SITUATION: Your child qualifies for a subsidized loan, but you need more money.

ACTION: Make sure your child applies for an unsubsidized Stafford too. After maxing out on the

subsidized loan, your child is eligible for up to another $2,000 a year in an unsubsidized Stafford.
Your school's financial aid office should automatically alert you to this, but the sad fact is that many
families leave Stafford money on the table every
year because they don't understand the rules about
unsubsidized loans.

SITUATION: What do you have to do to apply for
Stafford loans?

ACTION: There is one big requirement for Stafford
loans (and school financial aid): You must complete the Free Application for Federal Student
Aid (FAFSA). No FAFSA, no Staffords. It is not
a fun form to fill out, but spending a few hours
wading through all the financial disclosure is
worth it, trust me. Check with the school's financial aid office; they are set up to help you navigate
this process.

SITUATION: You have applied for subsidized and
unsubsidized Stafford loans, but you need even more
money.

ACTION: Apply for a Parental PLUS loan, another
federal loan program. The parent, not the student,
is the borrower. There is no income limit, and you
can borrow up to the full amount of college costs
minus any aid and other loans. The interest rate is

a fixed 8.5% for most borrowers. (It is 7.9% if the school is part of a program that has you borrow directly from the federal government, rather than using a third-party lender. Only 20% or so of schools are currently part of the Federal Direct Loan program. But as I write this, the Obama administration has proposed that all federal loans be administered directly. The financial aid office at your child's school will advise you on how to apply for a PLUS.) But I want to be clear: You apply for a PLUS only after your child has maxed out on the Staffords. A PLUS is a very good deal, but Staffords are even better given their lower interest rates. Staffords first. PLUS second.

SITUATION: You looked into a PLUS loan when your older child went to college a few years ago, but the repayment rules were too tough, so you're thinking it won't be an option for your younger children.

ACTION: Give the program a fresh look. In 2008 big changes were made to the PLUS program that make this a more viable and affordable option.

The big change is that you no longer must repay the loan while your child is in school; you can wait until your child finishes school. As I explain below this can be a huge help.

You will also find the qualifying rules for a PLUS to be less stringent than other types of loans. There is no FICO credit check per se to obtain a PLUS loan, but your credit history is reviewed to check for any "adverse" actions on your credit profile. Families that have declared bankruptcy in the past five years are not eligible for a PLUS loan. (If you are turned down for a PLUS loan, your child can qualify for larger Stafford loans.) PLUS loans are also a little bit forgiving of small cash-flow problems. The standard regulation is that you can qualify for a PLUS as long as you are no more than 90 days behind on mortgage or medical payments. For 2009 this rule was extended to 180 days. Please check my website for an update on the rules past 2009.

SITUATION: You want to take out a PLUS loan, but you know you can't afford to pay it back immediately.

ACTION: Don't worry—you don't have to. Thanks to legislation passed in 2008, parents no longer have to start repaying a PLUS loan within 60 days of receiving the money. You can now defer repayment until your child finishes school. That means you won't have to make loan payments during the four years when you are most likely using some of your monthly income to pay for school costs. The delay also means that families can make repayment of the PLUS a family affair: Legally, the parent is responsible for repayment of the loan, but having your child help with repayment will ease the burden.

Another reason I prefer PLUS loans over private loans is that in the event the parent dies or is permanently disabled, the debt is forgiven; private lenders are not required to forgive debt.

SITUATION: You want to help with a PLUS loan, but you are worried about handling the payments over the long term.

ACTION: Before you agree to take out a PLUS loan, you must have a serious talk with your child about how much you expect them to contribute to the eventual repayment of the PLUS. That is an important and honest conversation to have ahead of school. It may spur your child to push extra hard to earn the most money possible during the summer (or work part time during school) to build up some reserves. It might also put the cost for spring break in Cabo—definitely a "want," not a "need"—into perspective.

SITUATION: Your child wants you to cosign a private student loan.

ACTION: Forget private loans and use a PLUS if you plan to help your kid pay for school.

Students who want a private student loan need to have a FICO score of at least 680. Few teenagers have a FICO score. So lenders are now insisting that the student get a cosigner on the loan, and that person needs to have a strong FICO score.

Rather than cosign a private loan, you are far better off applying for a Parental PLUS loan and making it clear to your child that she is expected to repay some or all of the loan once she graduates. Part of my reason for relying on the PLUS program is a simple practical matter: In the wake of the financial crisis that began in 2008, it became much harder to obtain a private student loan. But even if the storm passes, the private loan skies part, and lenders start plying your kids with offers for easy private loans, I want you to say no. PLUS loans are usually a better choice over private loans. Private student loans have variable rates, and those rates can be 1% to 10% more than a benchmark index. Even if you initially qualify for a competitive interest rate (you'll need a FICO score above 720 to even have a shot), you run the risk of future rate hikes. I'll take the 8.5% fixed rate on the PLUS loan, thank you very much.

SITUATION: You just lost your job and you are in no position to help your kids with their college tuition. What do you do?

ACTION: Contact the financial aid office at each school immediately and let them know about the layoff. There may be more money—aid or loans—based on your changed financial status. But I want to be clear: No school is a bottomless pit, and the sad fact is that many schools—especially public universities—are feeling the economic pinch too. But chances are you may get some extra help from the school. And just to reiterate: Please make sure your child has maxed out on all available Stafford loans. At a maximum fixed rate of 6.8%, it is an affordable way to borrow for school.

You can also obtain a PLUS loan, assuming you are current on your bills, and you can defer payment until your child graduates. By then you should be back at work and your child can also contribute to the PLUS repayment. But I want to be very clear here: You must limit what you borrow to what you can truly afford. I encourage you to go to the College Board's website and use its online calculator to see what PLUS loans you take out today will cost to repay: http://apps.college board.com/fincalc/parpay.jsp. It is crucial that you go through this exercise with your newfound commitment to honesty front and center. If you will not be able to handle the repayment, do not take out the loan.

If not taking on debt is honestly what is best for you, you must not beat yourself up that you cannot continue to pay for school. I wish I could tell you to "do whatever is necessary" to keep your kid in school right now. But I don't traffic in wishful thinking; I am focused on the realistic actions you must take to ensure your long-term financial security. So here's the bottom line: You may need to tell your kids you can't keep paying for school now that your personal economic situation has changed. If that means your child needs to transfer to a less expensive school or take a year off to earn money to cover the costs himself, that is what needs to happen.

I understand how difficult that is to consider, but hard times require making hard choices. Taking on debt you can't afford is never smart; in today's world, with the economic outlook so bleak, you must not take on more than you can realistically handle.

SITUATION: You're about to graduate and you doubt you'll get a job that will pay enough to cover your student loan payments.

ACTION: If you have federal loans, there are a variety of programs you may qualify for that can make repayment more affordable. For example: The Income-Based Repayment Plan introduced in 2009 for federal student loans (though not PLUS loans) makes repayment affordable for graduates who pursue careers in traditionally lower-paying fields such as teaching and public service. The best move you can make is to show up for the exit interview with your financial aid office and learn about your options. You can also learn more about your repayment options at finaid.org.

The worst thing any recent graduate can do is assume they can "hide" or "ignore" their student loan debt until they get settled into a job and have the cash flow to handle payments. Big, big mistake. Fall behind on your student loans and you will ruin your credit profile. You need to understand that student loans are debts, and if you don't pay your debts it gets reported to the credit bureaus. Faster than you can say, "Wow, I am so screwed," you have a FICO score below 700. In my book, it's never okay to have a low FICO score, but in the aftermath of the financial crisis that began in 2009, it is flat-out dumb. Yes, dumb. In the past, even if you had a lousy FICO score you could still get what you wanted. The only hassle is that you would have to pay more for everything—a higher deposit for the cellphone, for example, or a higher rate for a car loan. But now a lousy FICO score means big trouble. Lenders, landlords, and even employers simply won't want to do business with you. In a world where everyone is trying to reduce their risk, a lousy FICO score brands you as a high risk.

And just to drive home this point: Even if you declare bankruptcy, your student loan debt in most cases will not be forgiven. This is debt you can't outrun.

SITUATION: The job market is terrible and you can't find a job, even with your brand-new degree. You have no clue how you will be able to start repaying your student loans.

ACTION: With federal loans, you can apply for an unemployment deferment; if you are working less than 30 hours a week, you will not have to start repayment. But again, you must *apply* for this deferment. If you simply don't pay, it is going to start showing up on your credit reports as a delinquency. If you have a subsidized federal loan, interest will not continue to build up during this deferment. If your loan is unsubsidized, interest does accrue. Your financial aid office can walk you through all your federal loan repayment options. You can also get help at finaid.org.

SITUATION: You graduated with debt from various student loans and you wonder if you should consolidate or not.

ACTION: Consolidating your federal loans is smart. The main advantage is that you can pile together all your loans from the four years of school into one mega-loan that requires just one monthly payment. This will likely keep your FICO score in good shape, because you will find it easier to stay on top of things with a single payment.

The fixed consolidation rate for all Stafford loans issued after July 1, 2006, is 6.8%.

SITUATION: You graduated with private student loans. Can you consolidate them and defer payments?

ACTION: With private student loans you have limited options. You are basically at the mercy of your lender's repayment policy, and they are not required to grant any deferments. It's completely at their discretion.

8

Protecting Your Family and Yourself

New Rules for New Times

In previous chapters of this book I explained how to protect your money from being decimated by risk. You must have an emergency savings fund, and it must be in a federally insured bank or credit union. Your retirement and college funds must have an age-appropriate mix of stocks, bonds, and cash.

Those strategies go a long way toward increasing your family's security. The final piece of risk management focuses on how to protect your family from being decimated by the risk of the unknown. Bad things happen, and when they do, it is painful—it doesn't matter who you are or where things stand in your life.

Let's start with job risk. By the fall of 2009, the base unemployment rate of 10.2% was more than double the average in 2007. Add in the legions of part-time, underemployed workers, and the unemployed/underemployed rate reaches 17.5%. One out of nearly every six Americans who wants to work full-time can't. That, of course, isn't a permanent situation. As we pull out of the recession, we will likely see the unemployment rate decline. But there is the very real possibility that the recovery, when it comes, could be a "jobless" recovery; businesses skittish to overinvest amid forecasts of moderate domestic economic growth could well be slow to hire. That's just one reason I recommend an eight-month emergency cash fund. It may take a very long time to get back to work.

Illness and injury are also looming risks that must be planned for. As I write this in the fall of 2009, Congress is debating and negotiating health care reform that would extend coverage to millions of uninsured Americans as well as make it easier for millions more to hold on to coverage they live in fear of losing. Yet any new legislation will take years to be fully implemented. The bill that narrowly passed the House in early November 2009 sets a 2013 date for enacting broader coverage. In the meantime, you can't let your family live with the risk of staying uninsured or underinsured.

And let's talk about another sunny topic: the

prospect that you could die prematurely. I know it is excruciating to contemplate. There is no plan or action that will alleviate the pain your family will endure, but you can most definitely alleviate their financial stress—by making sure there is ample life insurance if you have yet to build other assets they can rely on, and by creating the essential must-have documents of a will and revocable living trust.

There is no way to insulate your family from bad news, but what is wholly in your control is how well prepared you and your family are to weather hard times. The New Rules for Protecting Your Family and Yourself are simply a recognition that risk is not just in the stock market and the real estate market. It can descend on your family at any time. Now that your eyes are open and you are aware of the risks out there, isn't it time to make sure your family is as protected as possible for whatever "what if" may strike?

What you must do

- Build a substantial savings account today so you will be okay if you are laid off.
- Do not—repeat, do not—go without health insurance.
- Shop for private health insurance if you are laid off; it is often less expensive than COBRA.
- Purchase an affordable term life insurance policy if anyone is dependent on your income.

■ Make sure you have all your estate-planning documents in order.

Your Action Plan:
Protecting Your Family and Yourself

SITUATION: You are worried you may lose your job.

ACTION: Prepare for it. As of October 2009 the unemployment rate is at 10.2%, the highest level in more than 26 years. Even if the economy has improved by the time you read this, I want you to remember what happened in 2009 and use it as all the motivation you need to protect your family in the event we hit another rough period. As I always say, hope for the best, prepare for the worst. And the best way to protect your family is to know that you will still be able to pay the bills if you are ever laid off.

This makes it imperative that you build an emergency savings account that can cover your family's living expenses for eight months. I know that is a lot, but you have got to start saving as much as you can right now. In "Action Plan: Spending," I review the steps you and your family can take to rein in your spending today so you have more money to put into a safe savings account.

And if you flew past the Action Plans for credit and real estate, I want to make sure you are up to speed on the fact that you may not be able to tap your credit card or a home equity line of credit to pay your family's bills in the event you are laid off.

You also want to start your job hunt right now—while you still have your current job. Network like crazy, show up at industry conferences, and take a look at job postings in your field. If there is any specific skill mentioned that you are not up to speed on, get yourself schooled on it ASAP. Employers aren't interested in hiring someone who meets 80% of their needs when they have such a large pool to choose from that they can find the person who meets 100% of their needs. Make sure that person is you.

SITUATION: You figure you will get by on unemployment benefits if you are laid off.

ACTION: You will still need to supplement that money with your own savings. The reality is that your maximum unemployment benefit typically will replace less than 50% of your lost wages. There is also a time limit to those payouts; 26 weeks is the standard amount of time you are eligible to collect unemployment. In harsh economic times, Congress can vote to extend the benefit period for an additional 13 weeks. (Unemployment is handled by your state, based on general standards set by federal law.)

To find out your state's rules, go to www.service
locator.org and click on the Unemployment Benefits link.

SITUATION: You plan to use your credit card or HELOC to cover your expenses if you lose your job.

ACTION: You must have money set aside in a regular bank savings account or money market account. There is no guarantee that the lines of credit you have relied on in the past will be available when you need them. The only way to protect yourself and your family is to have your own savings set aside in a federally insured bank or credit union. You also need to appreciate that lenders are one step ahead of you. If they are worried that an economic slowdown could cause you to lose your job, they aren't going to just shrug it off. They know if that happens you will then use your credit card or HELOC to cover your bills, and because you don't have a job, that increases the likelihood that you won't be able to keep up with the payments on that borrowed money. So, to head off this problem, lenders will cut back on what they allow customers to borrow in tough times.

The only safe alternative is to have cash set aside in a savings account.

SITUATION: You plan to make early withdrawals from your 401(k) if you are laid off and can't pay your bills.

ACTION: Try as hard as you can not to touch your retirement savings. What seems like a reasonable action to help you get through problems today will devastate your long-term security. You need that money for retirement; spend it today and you will have less tomorrow. And don't tell me you will worry about that later, or you will boost your savings when you get another job. Even the best of intentions to make up for the withdrawals can run into harsh realities: Your next job may not pay enough to allow you to save to make up for your early withdrawal. (That said, if you feel you are out of options and need to raid your retirement funds to get by, please review my advice in "Action Plan: Retirement" about how you may be able to take money out of your 401[k] without having to pay the typical 10% early withdrawal penalty.)

There is one important action I want you to take with your 401(k) if you are laid off: Roll over the money into an IRA at a brokerage or mutual fund company. As I explain in "Action Plan: Retirement," rolling your money into an IRA gives you access to the best low-cost mutual funds and ETFs, rather than limiting yourself to the investment choices in your 401(k).

SITUATION: You don't have money to set aside in savings.

ACTION: Get serious about finding ways to come up with real savings—right now. This is nonnegotiable: You must build up a savings reserve. In "Action Plan: Spending," I explain how you and your family can (and must) adjust to the new realities to find ways to reduce your expenses—or increase your income—so you have money to put toward important financial goals. There is nothing more important than building an emergency savings fund that can carry your family for eight months.

SITUATION: You dropped health insurance coverage through your employer in 2009 because it was too expensive and you are healthy.

ACTION: Get insurance now. If you can't get it from your employer, shop for your own policy. I don't care how healthy you are today. It's tomorrow I am worried about, and you and I both know a serious accident or sudden illness is always a possibility. Remember: Hope for the best, prepare for the worst. You need to understand that many of the families that end up filing for bankruptcy did so because they had unexpected medical bills that were impossible to pay off. Having health insurance reduces your financial burden if anyone in your family becomes severely ill or injured. Now, the truth is, insurance doesn't absolutely protect you from bankruptcy. The sad fact is that even people with insurance end up in bankruptcy because of high copays and costs that aren't covered. But the point is that insurance offers you some protection, whereas without insurance you have no protection.

I appreciate how expensive it is. Employers have been increasing charges to employees for their coverage; that can mean higher premiums, higher copays, or reductions in the scope of coverage. This is happening because health insurance costs keep rising at a rapid rate and companies are hard-pressed to shoulder the cost, and also because businesses feel the pressure to boost earnings (or minimize losses). Shifting more benefit costs onto employees helps the corporate bottom line.

Regardless of cost, you must have some insurance. If your old plan is too expensive, you should have shopped around for less expensive options within the plan. The reality is that because you turned down coverage during the open-enrollment period, typically in the fall, you may be shut out from restarting your coverage until the next enrollment period. (Certain exceptions apply for new employees and employees with life-changing events, such as a divorce or job change; check with your human resources department.) If that's the case, I am asking you to get short-term coverage through a private plan until you are eligible to get back on your company's plan.

SITUATION: You want to wait to see what options you may have if Washington passes health care reform.

ACTION: As I write this in November of 2009, it looks as if there may indeed be health care reform. But I don't want you to wait for Washington to save you. You need protection right now. Even if legislation is passed, extended coverage may not be effective until 2013. You can always drop it if and when we have reform in place. That's one nice thing about health insurance: You pay your premium monthly, rather than annually. So you can drop the coverage whenever you want.

SITUATION: You don't know where to find affordable health insurance.

ACTION: Go to ehealthinsurance.com, the largest online resource for health insurance. If you prefer to work with an agent, the National Association of Health Underwriters (nahu.org) has an online search tool to give you leads on agents who help clients find individual health insurance policies. As you shop, realize that the group plan at your old job probably included a full menu of broad coverage—including mental health and maternity benefits, prescription drug coverage, and so on—that you may not need. Shop for a policy that provides only the specific coverage you need to keep your premium cost as low as possible.

SITUATION: You were laid off and can't afford the COBRA rate for your company's health insurance.

ACTION: Shop for less expensive health insurance. But do not—repeat, do not—go without health insurance. You can't afford to be uninsured. What if someone in your family becomes ill or is in a serious accident? Ehealthinsurance.com has created a website specifically for people who have been laid off; it includes a calculator to help you see what alternatives to COBRA might cost: www .ehealthinsurance.com/ehi/health-insurance/ cobra-learning-center.html.

SITUATION: You wonder whether you should keep the health insurance from your former employer or shop for a private plan.

ACTION: In many cases, a private plan will be less expensive than staying on your company plan. Here's what you need to know: Every employer with more than 20 employees that offers health insurance is required by the federal COBRA regulation to allow employees who've been laid off to stay on the company plan for 18 months, with one very big catch: The employee is responsible for 100% of the cost of the plan, as well as an extra 2% to cover administration costs. That is not just 100% of your normal premium when you were an employee, but 100% of the total cost, including what your employer used to pay on your behalf. So that can be a lot more than you were paying as an employee.

PLEASE NOTE: *A special federal law passed in 2009 reduced the employee's share of the COBRA premium to just 35% of the total cost for the first nine months you have COBRA coverage. (Your employer receives a government tax credit for the other 65%.) This special law was in place for people laid off between September 2008 and December 31, 2009. Please check my website for updates on whether this provision has been extended beyond 2009.*

SITUATION: You were let go and you have a preexisting health condition. You worry that you will not qualify for a private plan or it will be too expensive.

ACTION: Stay on the company plan through COBRA, but get a private insurance plan for your family. Assuming your family is in good health, the cost of a private insurance plan for them will be less than continuing their coverage through COBRA.

At the same time, find a health insurance broker with extensive experience working with clients with preexisting conditions. (Go to nahu.org to find a list of agents in your area.) Different insurers have different policies; you want to work with someone who will shop around to locate a plan that may work for you. If you can't secure a private policy, you may have to opt for coverage offered through your state. This can often be very costly, so it is definitely to be used as a last resort. You can find links to your state insurance department at naic.org (National Association of Insurance Commissioners).

SITUATION: You were told your state doesn't offer coverage to all residents.

ACTION: Stay on COBRA for as long as possible. I am sorry to say that there are indeed many states that do not have any last-resort coverage available for residents who can't qualify for an individual private policy. Just five states—Maine, Massachusetts, New Jersey, New York, and Vermont—have programs in place that offer guaranteed insurance at all times and to all residents. In Rhode Island, North Carolina, and Virginia (and in some instances Pennsylvania), you may be able to get last-resort coverage if you have been turned down for private policies. Contact your state health insurance commissioner's office to find out what's offered where you live; or look up your state's health insurance options on www.coverageforall .org.

SITUATION: You lost your job and the only new job you have been offered doesn't come with health benefits.

ACTION: Do not base your job search on health benefits. Take the job and shop for your own individual policy or continue on your old employer's plan through COBRA. But you need to choose COBRA coverage within 60 days of being notified you were COBRA-eligible; if more time has already passed, you have lost your right to stay on your old employer's plan.

SITUATION: You were laid off and want to go back to school so you can change careers.

ACTION: Get a job; school can wait. I am all for changing careers—hey, I spent my first seven years after college working as a waitress—but I am always suspicious when I hear someone tell me they want to go back to school right after they were laid off. It becomes this nice safety blanket to wrap yourself in, rather than dealing with a tough job market. But if you haven't really thought through what your new career is and you haven't figured out a financial plan for how you will pay for school, then it becomes a lousy idea. What are you going to live on while you go back to school? Don't think you can touch your emergency savings plan. That's for emergencies. Going back to school is not an emergency. It is a choice. Plan on taking out loans? Okay, but again, what are you going to live on while you are in school? Credit cards? That's never a good idea.

A career change can be the best move you will ever make, but it requires careful planning. I say focus on getting another job right now, even if it's just for a year or so, while you carefully plan your new career and build up your savings so you can afford to go back to school.

SITUATION: You were laid off after 20 years with the same company. You are having a hard time finding a new job at the same salary and level of responsibility.

ACTION: Be realistic. What you made at your last job is somewhat irrelevant. What employers are willing to pay today for the job they have today is what really matters. For people who have spent a lot of time at one company, this is a tough concept to accept. But it is vitally important.

People who have been with the same company for many years may have developed special skills particular to that company or industry, and they may have been well compensated for that exper-

tise. But there is no guarantee your next employer
needs those very skills or values them as much as
your former employer did. If you have the financial flexibility to wait for a perfect offer, that's
your call. But I want you to be realistic. How you
value yourself and how the market values you may
well be different. Don't hold out for an offer that
may never materialize. I am all for valuing yourself and what you do, but not at the cost of jeopardizing your family's financial security. Realize that
the longer you are out of work the harder it may be
to sell yourself and your résumé to prospective
employers. A good job; perhaps not the perfect
job, may be the best move for you, if only for now.
If you end up needing to take a job that pays less
than your prior job, that's just another challenge
to meet. In "Action Plan: Spending," I have advice
on how families can make more out of less.

SITUATION: You received a four-month severance
package and plan on taking two months off to relax
and regroup before beginning your job hunt.

ACTION: I wouldn't do it. Sure, take a few weeks
to decompress and refresh. But you need to start
the job hunt sooner rather than later. It could very
well take a lot longer than you expect.

SITUATION: You have life insurance through your
employer. What happens to it if you are laid off?

ACTION: Whether you're laid off or not, I want you to get your own coverage. I have never recommended relying on employer-provided life insurance. If your employer provides coverage for free, chances are you are woefully uninsured; employer-provided life insurance is typically equal to one or two times your annual salary. I recommend 10 to 25 times to fully protect your family. Even if you buy extra insurance through your employer, it can often be more expensive than what you can get on your own; that's because you are paying a group rate based on all employees—young, old, healthy, not so healthy.

Another problem is that when you are laid off you eventually (within 18 months) need to convert to your own policy. And there is no guarantee the insurer who offered you group coverage will offer you an individual policy or one that is the least costly.

SITUATION: You haven't bought life insurance because you can't afford to.

ACTION: If there are people in your life who are dependent in any way on the income you earn, then you can't afford not to have life insurance. Seriously, what will happen to them if you die prematurely? Be it young kids, older parents who require financial assistance, or a sibling you help out—if you do not have sufficient assets your dependents can live off of, you need life insurance.

I think you will also be surprised by how remarkably affordable term life insurance is. A $1 million 20-year term policy for a healthy 45-year-old woman can cost less than $125 a month.

SITUATION: You're not sure if you should get term insurance or whole-life insurance.

ACTION: For the vast majority of us, term insurance is all that is needed.

As its name implies, term insurance is a policy for a specific period of time, the term. If you die during the term, your beneficiaries receive the death benefit (payout) from the insurer. And here's what you need to know: Chances are you have only a temporary need for life insurance. You need insurance while your kids are young and dependent on you; once they are adults, they will be financially independent. You need life insurance if you have yet to build up other assets (home equity, retirement investments) that will support your dependents when you die. Once you have those assets in place, it is less likely your surviving spouse or partner would need income from a life insurance policy in the event you pass away first.

Many insurance agents will tell you term is not enough. They will tell you that you want a permanent policy that never expires. Permanent policies come in a few different flavors: whole life, universal life, and variable life. I want to repeat: If your need for insurance is temporary—say, just until your youngest is through college—you absolutely do not need a permanent policy. And you will needlessly spend tens of thousands of dollars more for a permanent policy than a term policy.

SITUATION: You don't know how to shop for term insurance.

ACTION: You can shop online; selectquote.com and accuquote.com specialize in working with individuals who need term insurance. You will be asked to fill out a comprehensive worksheet of your income and assets as well as your expenses and debt. How much life insurance you need depends on those factors. If you want to be absolutely sure your family will be financially well off if you die prematurely, I would consider buying a policy with a death benefit equal to 25 times your family's annual income needs. Full disclosure: That is more than double what many insurance agents may recommend. You can indeed help your family tremendously with a smaller amount of coverage, but I am asking you to consider 25× for absolute peace of mind. If your death benefit is 25× your family's annual needs, they can take the payout and invest in conservative bonds (such as municipal bonds) and live off the principal amount. If your death benefit is smaller, they will eventually need to dip into the principal and it could sharply reduce how long the money lasts.

SITUATION: You have a term life insurance policy, but you're worried your insurer will go out of business.

ACTION: Know that your state insurance department will be looking out for you. The insurance department oversees a state guaranty association that provides coverage (up to the limits spelled out by state law) for policyholders of insurers licensed to do business in their state. In the case of life insurance, the guaranty association and state insurance commissioner will aim to have a healthy company take over the policies, so you will not see a change. You can find out how the guaranty system safety net operates in your state by visiting the National Organization of Life & Health Insurance Guaranty Associations' website: www.nolhga.com.

SITUATION: You aren't sure what estate-planning documents you need.

ACTION: You need a revocable living trust with an incapacity clause, as well as a will. Read that again. A will is not enough. I want you to also have a revocable living trust. And you need two durable powers of attorney—one for health care and one for finances. A power of attorney designates someone you trust to carry out your affairs in the event you become unable to handle matters on your own. Your health care power of attorney will be your "voice" in medical decisions if you are unable to speak for yourself, and the financial power of attorney can handle your bills and financial affairs. You also need an advance directive that spells out your wishes for the level of medical care you want should you become too ill to speak for yourself.

9

ACTION PLAN

Kids and Money

New Rules for New Times

For all the uncertainty we face in the world, there is one unwavering, unquestionable, and irrefutable fact of life: You would do anything for your children. It is both your job and your honor as a parent to care for your kids. And so it should be.

But the recent financial crisis has raised a new challenge for many parents. For a variety of reasons you now find yourself needing to change the way your family spends money. A layoff. A diminished 401(k). Lost home equity. The sobering realization that a lifestyle fueled by credit card debt is no longer sustainable.

In your heart you know that the way forward requires a new approach to spending and saving. You also know that it is all for the best; once and for all, you are going to take control of your financial life with a focus on building lasting security. Yet you are on edge about how to sell this new way of life to your children. You don't want to disappoint them, you don't want to say no, you simply won't ask them to pay any price for changes in your circumstances.

I need you to step back and consider the unintended damage you are inflicting on your children. I want to be clear that I am not challenging or questioning your motivation; there is nothing more primal than nurturing a child. My sense, though, is that many parents are falling short on doing just that. Actions that you believe are loving and supportive—actions that are rooted in the best of intentions—can still, ultimately, be so wrong.

When you fail to instill sound money principles in your children while they are under your roof, you increase the chance that they will flounder when they have to make their way in the world. I could fill a year's worth of my CNBC show with young adults who are so frustrated that they didn't better understand credit card debt, what it takes to build a strong credit score, and how to budget. They come to me for help because their parents dropped the ball. Look, I am not suggesting that teaching your kids about money is the most important lesson. Please. You and I are in absolute agreement that raising children to have a solid moral and ethical center is paramount. But don't you want them to also be happy and secure? Well, that moves money front and center in your parenting duties. The quality of your children's lives will in large part be a function of the quality of their money choices. But they need to learn right from wrong; preferably before they learn from painful experience.

I ask that you step back and seriously consider every lesson and message you are imparting. Do you—or did you—ever say to your young kids, "I wish I could stay at home and be with you instead of going off to work, but I have to make money." Sound like basic parental love? You could not be more wrong. You have just telegraphed that work and money are bad! As if work is the enemy that keeps you from your children, instead of the means by which you provide your family with a comfortable, secure life. Of course you wish you had more time to spend with your family, but why demonize work as a way of expressing a loving feeling? It's not exactly a great start to teaching them great money (and work) habits.

The good news for you is that your kids want money lessons! A 2009 survey by Charles Schwab & Co. asked more than 1,200 young adults between the ages of 23 and 28 how prepared they felt to make good financial choices. Fewer than 20% reported they felt well prepared to invest and save, just one in five said they were confident they knew how to manage debt wisely, and only one third reported they had a handle on how to live within their means. Those results weren't surprising, coming on the heels of an earlier Schwab survey of teens between the ages of 13 and 18. In that, just one in three teens believed "their parents/guardians are concerned with making sure they are learning the basics of smart money management," and just one-third of children said they understood why their parents make the financial decisions they do. Only 20% of the teens surveyed said their parents had "taught me how to invest money wisely to make it grow."

Don't look to schools to impart this lesson; the sad fact is our educational system has no established protocols or plans to prepare today's children to manage their financial lives. It's all on you, parents! Your kids are literally looking to you for help.

Now, I realize for some of you this may entail simultaneously learning while teaching; your kids may not yet have great money habits because you haven't exactly had a handle on matters yourself. And as with many habits—good and bad—your kids learn by example: the example you set. So teaching your kids about money presents an opportunity to embark on a concerted family project: You will tackle your new financial planning as a team.

More good news is that the financial crisis is

one big, very real moment, ready to be explained. No need for hypotheticals and "just trust me" talks. The turmoil in the world outside your door, and perhaps inside your own family's finances, provides plenty of real-life examples. There is no shortage of entry points to talk about all facets of personal finance, from borrowing to budgeting to investing. Do not shy away from the hard topics, or think your kids don't need to know that you are dealing with a financial challenge. I find it so frustrating that parents think they should shield their children from what is going on. I can't tell you how disrespectful that is of your kids. As if they can't see, hear, and sense for themselves what is going on in the world, and in their very own homes. Just because you don't talk about it openly doesn't mean they aren't aware of it; they may even be afraid of what's going on, but don't know how to ask the right questions to seek reassurance. Silence here is so dangerous. They need to talk about it; *you* need to talk about it. Of course the conversation you have with a 6-year-old is far different than the one you have with a 16-year-old, but at every age there is an appropriate conversation to be had.

Your message and tone should inspire confidence and calm, not fear. That your family may decide to spend less in order to save more is not about "making do with less," it is about making your lives more secure. In the process of making smart choices for your family today, you are imparting the lessons your kids are craving.

To be sure, if the spending spigot has been wide open for years, the New Rules for Kids and Money are going to take some getting used to—for you, and for the kids. Everyone will need time and encouragement, and maybe some patience, as you transition to your new money-wise habits. But you are in the lead here. Your children are sponges; their attitudes are your attitudes. Their actions are a reflection of your actions. Kids do what you do, not what you say. If you make this a journey born of guilt, remorse, and failure, that's the lesson they will take from you and carry with them the rest of their lives. Or you can embrace your new money habits with a sense of clarity and purpose and hope that what you are committing to today will benefit all of you, every day, from here on out.

What you must do

- Take responsibility for teaching your kids how to handle money.
- In an age-appropriate manner, talk to your kids about changes in your financial situation. Silence is damaging.
- Give your children tangible lessons in budgeting; have them help you pay the bills and, when appropriate, give them a budget to manage for themselves.

- Teach your children about credit card debt and the power of compound interest before they graduate from high school.
- Make *your* retirement saving a priority. It will be the greatest gift for your grown children.

Your Action Plan: Kids and Money

SITUATION: You don't know how to explain to your children that you must spend less now. It feels like you are punishing them, and that's making you feel worse than you already do.

ACTION: Talk about your goals—what you are moving toward—rather than focusing on what you are leaving behind. Your attitude is key here. If you approach this with guilt or a sense that you are failing your children, you are literally telegraphing to them that they should be disappointed and angry.

I am not talking about spin for spin's sake; your goal is not to manipulate your children into thinking this is all fabulous news. Acknowledge that you so wish there was plenty of money for everything you and they could ever want. But that's not where your family is at right now, so you are going to focus your spending on true *needs*, not *wants*. That could well entail its own conversation about what is a need (electricity, food) and what is a want (a $100 pair of sneakers rather than a perfectly functional $40 pair).

Respect your children and explain the "why" behind the fact that you can't afford three after-school programs this year, or why you are scaling back the cable service, or why you will not be buying them a car when they get their driver's license. Not because they are bad or undeserving, or because you are bad. But because life throws curveballs from time to time. And right now your family needs to work hard to spend less so you can focus on new goals. Maybe that goal is making sure your emergency savings can last through a layoff, maybe that goal is paying off credit card debt, maybe that goal is knowing how important it is to save some money for the future.

SITUATION: Your eight-year-old came home and said his best friend's dad was laid off, then he heard two parents at the park talking about how much "trouble" we are all in, and now he is panicked.

ACTION: Talk to him. Really talk to him. Saying "Don't worry" is not talking. It is dismissive and dangerous. Your kid has already announced his worry, so now it's up to you to work through it with him.

The level of specificity depends on your child's age. An eight-year-old doesn't have the capacity to digest a discussion of Wall Street greed, lax regulation, and easy lending standards. But he can most definitely grasp a conversation about making smart choices and making bad choices, and that there were a lot of bad choices made that we now need to fix. Reassure him. Even if you are scared yourself, do not let that seep into your conversation and your actions. Your child needs to know that no matter what happens, you have a plan, and you have his back.

SITUATION: You don't know how to tell your kids that you have been laid off.

ACTION: Ever tell your kids that honesty is the best policy? Great—now follow your own advice. If you have a partner, first sit down and give it a dress rehearsal; you want to run through this conversation first without the kids present.

Once you sit down with the kids, be calm and reassuring. Don't downplay it by saying it is "no big deal." It is indeed a very big deal. But it is something you will cope with. Make sure young children understand exactly what has happened; often language we think is clear—laid off, let go, fired—is confusing in itself. Explain that you had a job, but you no longer have that job. Make it clear that you have a plan; that you are working on getting a new job; that it may take time, but you are in control of things.

Then you need to address how the layoff may affect your children. If you have money stashed in an emergency savings fund and you got a great package when you were let go, maybe the immediate impact to your kids will be minimal. But I know that for many of you the financial stress is immediate and harsh. Again, be honest here. If your children are teens, spell out that you will be looking for ways to trim the family spending for the duration.

Give teenagers space to be scared and confused, and maybe a little bit angry. Not a ton of space, but enough to allow them to adjust to the news that their life has changed too. Just as you needed time to get over the hurt and shock of being laid off, you need to let them work through the emotion of this curveball.

You might not want to get into specifics in the first conversation, but plan a follow-up soon after to talk about how you will be making adjustments as a family. A generic "We need to cut back" is not the way to go. Share specifics so they can have a tangible sense of what will help. Maybe this will resonate for your family: *You know, when we go out to the movies it's great fun, but for the four of us it costs $45 in tickets, then another $15 for popcorn and sodas. That's $60. Instead of going to the movies it would be good for us to rent a movie from Netflix or On Demand* *for a few dollars and make popcorn in the microwave. We can save $50 right there. That's a big help.*

If your layoff necessitates cutting back on household help such as a gardener, housekeeper, or dog walker, those are all tasks where any child can pitch in. You may get some groans, but if you position this as a family financial project I bet they will soon come around and appreciate their ability to contribute.

SITUATION: You are so stressed about money you worry that your kids can feel—and hear—the stress.

ACTION: You are right to worry. This is a big test of parenting. How you handle this stress telegraphs lessons in navigating through hardship. That's hugely important, but studies have also found that how parents handle financial stress can literally affect their children's development. If you are strung out about money worries, that is going to have an impact on the way you relate to your family. If you are feeling depressed or your relationship becomes unstable under the money strain, it can create an unstable environment for your children, and that, in time, can expose them to even greater problems, such as floundering in school and substance abuse.

I realize these are trying times for many of you. But just do your best to stay strong and focused for your kids. Set your sights on getting them through the tough time and ensuring that they stay on a path to becoming everything they deserve to be, and everything you so want for them.

SITUATION: After being out of work for six months, you have finally found a good job. The only problem is it is 400 miles away, requiring your family to relocate, and you know the kids are not going to uproot easily.

ACTION: Life happens. That said, give them time and space to panic. Honor and respect their emotions, but do not feel guilty.

Then look for ways to help them make the transition. While you may be eager to have everyone relocate with you as soon as possible, consider having your kids stay put with your spouse or partner so they can finish out the school year. That gives all of you time to ease into the move. Make finding a new home a family affair; do not buy or rent something and then present it to the kids as a done deal. Sure it's ultimately your call, but asking them to help you find the right place makes them a part of the process. The move is happening with them, not just to them.

You might also consider booking a return trip to your old home after you leave for good. Or arrange for each child's best friend to come visit you in your new city. You can help them by creating bridges between old and new.

SITUATION: You find it too hard to say no to your daughter when she asks you for money to buy trendy clothes to keep up with her friends. But with your credit line cut and your interest rate high you are no longer willing—or able—to keep charging every "want" on your credit card.

ACTION: Needs must be separated from wants. It is your job to provide for every need, and if it fits your budget, throw in a few wants along the way too. But let me be clear, when I say "fits your budget," I mean you already have the eight-month emergency savings fund tucked away, you are saving for retirement, and you don't have any credit card debt. If any of those aren't in place, you are not allowed to give in on a "want" for your child.

If your child is upset by this, it's time to introduce her to the notion of earning the money for the purchase through either a real job, such as babysitting, or chores around the house. If your child is already earning an allowance, come up with additional responsibilities for her to earn extra money. No freebies. No giveaways. E-A-R-N is the operative word here.

SITUATION: Every time you go shopping with the kids, you end up spending way more than you intended.

ACTION: Whether you are at the mall or shopping online, always have a list of what you need, and stick to that list! If your child loves to shop and hops from store to store, do not let him make a single purchase until he has cased all the possibilities. If your list said you were buying three pairs of pants, then it's up to him to choose the three. Not four. Not five. Three. Plain and simple.

SITUATION: You want to start teaching your six-year-old about money, but you aren't sure if he is ready for allowance.

ACTION: It's not whether he is ready for an allowance, it is whether you are ready to step up and begin teaching the invaluable lesson of earning money for work. That's the only way you can impart the value of money. It makes me nuts that parents just hand out allowances as some sort of birthright. What a squandered opportunity to teach your child about being responsible and productive, and that it takes work to get money to buy what you want.

I am not a fan of the fixed weekly allowance. Rather, I would discuss a set of chores you expect your child to perform during any given week. I recommend coming up with two sets of chores for your child: uncompensated and compensated. Uncompensated chores are the jobs we all do as part of our contribution to being a family. For a small child, that could be something as simple as making her

bed or tossing her dirty laundry in the hamper instead of leaving it strewn around their room. Then
you need to clearly spell out chores that you consider
worthy of compensation—those that go "above and
beyond." For little ones, it may be something as simple as helping to deliver all the clean folded laundry
to the correct room. Coach them during the week so
they can learn what it takes to earn their allowance;
don't punish them by announcing at the end of the
week that because they didn't do their chores they
won't get paid. It's so important to make this a positive experience, not a punitive one.

But you do need to be clear: If a child ultimately
does not accomplish his or her chores, you must
not pay her the allowance. Remember, this is an
early lesson in understanding what it takes to earn
money. You are instilling a work ethic here, and to
reward children for work not done sends the wrong
message. No work, no allowance. But that just
raises the stakes for you to help them turn it around
the following week. As I said, keep it positive, and
make the weekly allowance conversation a ritual.
Make it as clockwork as a paycheck.

SITUATION: Your 14-year-old blows through her
weekly allowance in three days and starts hitting you
up like an ATM on day four.

ACTION: Shift your child to receiving her allowance every two weeks, and make it clear there is

no coming back to the Bank of Mom and Dad for more. This is Intro to Living on a Budget. She needs to figure out how to make her money last to the end of the two-week period. When she hits 16, shift to a monthly schedule. Sit with your kids and figure out where their money goes and make suggestions of ways to discipline their spending. Talk about saving up for a long-term goal, such as a laptop. Work out a schedule of savings. Teach your children how to budget on your dime and they will be more likely to budget wisely in a few years when they are on their own. The kids who don't know how to budget and live within their means are usually the ones who end up saddled with thousands of dollars in credit card debt in college.

And at the risk of stating the obvious: Tell her to get a job if she is coming up short. You are not to create more house chores simply to find a way to funnel more money to your kid so she can buy whatever she has to have this moment. It's time for a *job*. And no advancing money to her once she has the job. She needs to go through the process of saving what she earns so she can eventually afford whatever it is she wants. The more time and effort it takes, the more valued the purchase will be.

SITUATION: Your teenaged kids have no clue what it costs to keep the family running, but you aren't sure how to teach a little without overburdening them at the same time.

ACTION: Make bill paying a family affair from time to time with your teens. Whether it is literally writing the check or handling the clicks with online bill pay, let your kids see the utility bill, the credit card bill, and, God help us, the cellphone bill. You aren't looking to make your kids feel guilty; this is simply an opportunity to open their eyes to what it takes to function.

Speaking of cellphones, when you decide to give your child one, don't pass up the opportunity for a great financial lesson. Even if you are simply adding a child to an existing plan, let him know what his "share" of the bill is. I would recommend that you increase his chores and responsibilities around the house to offset the cost of his phone. Again, you are not denying him; you are taking advantage of a natural way to teach him that nothing is free. And any excess minutes he runs up need to come out of his own allowance.

You can also make the bill-paying exercise a challenge for your kids to help the family save more. If you're like most families, lights are left turned on, showers can run forever, and everyone wants the heat cranked up in the winter and the air-conditioning blasting in the summer. Tell your kids that if they can get themselves—and the whole family—to reduce your bill by at least 10% (or more; you set the goal) you will pay them half of the savings.

SITUATION: Birthday parties and holiday celebrations are out of control in your kid's circles. You don't want her to feel out of place, so you spend more on parties and gifts than you can truly afford.

ACTION: You have a simple choice to make: You can do what is right, or you can do what is easy. I know it's not easy, but there is no legitimate rationale for spending $1,000 on a kid's birthday if that $1,000 will go on a credit card with 18% interest. Whether you scale back the guest list or go for a low-cost party—a slumber party only costs you a few pizzas and one night's sleep and sanity—there are indeed ways to celebrate without breaking the bank. The choice is yours. And if you are about to tell me that you just can't do that to your kid, I am going to ask you how it is that you think going into debt to pay for something unaffordable is good for her in any way.

The same honesty must be used when you are buying presents for your child, or for a party your child is attending. Buy a gift your family can afford. It is irrelevant what other kids get or give. Can't imagine putting your kid in this situation? Please. Here's what I want you to imagine: By playing this costly financial charade, you are setting your child up to be a financial mess as an adult. Let's review: Your kids do as you do. If your gift buying telegraphs that it is okay to spend more than you have to spend to keep up with the Joneses, then you'd better believe your kid is going to have lousy spending habits as an adult.

Another thing I want to point out: If you (or your kids) think that friends judge you by your possessions or the price of your gifts, you need an Action Plan for getting new friends or developing some self-esteem. Before the financial crisis it was easy to deceive yourself that you could spend beyond your means. That's no longer the case. If the financial crisis forces you to refocus on what is important—love, support, friendship—and let go of the trappings of living beyond your means, I say: Good for you. You and your kids will ultimately be happier for living more honestly.

SITUATION: Your child was given a gift of a lot of money, and wants to spend it all on videogames and mall crawls.

ACTION: Denied. I don't care whether the money was a bar/bat mitzvah gift or a generous check at Christmas from Grandma and Grandpa, you are not to squander this opportunity to teach good money habits by letting your child squander the money. You are to introduce the 10-10-80 Rule:

■ **10% of the gift is your child's to spend as he pleases.** Do not judge how the money is spent.

For this to work, you have to be supportive of every step of the plan.

- **10% of the gift is to be donated to a charity of your child's choosing.** Don't impose your beliefs; instead, help your child think about the causes he considers important. If you will be writing the check on behalf of your child, make it clear that the donation is clearly made on his behalf. You want him to receive the acknowledgment (and all the follow-up mail!).

- **80% is to be saved or invested by you for the benefit of your child.** Explain that you are not taking the money away from him, you are merely overseeing the management of that money for his future benefit. It's time to start explaining the high cost of your child's needs and wants— not as a guilt trip, but as an honest and truthful education about what it costs to, well, live life. And that's why 80% of the gift will be earmarked for some of his future expenses, be it an incredible summer trip when he is older, an expensive specialty camp, or even dorm room furnishings. Make it clear that this is about creating more for him—by saving, rather than spending, the bulk of his gift. Check in with your child once or twice a year to show him the status of his 80%. Use this as the great opportunity it is to talk about saving and goals, and the cost of providing so many of the experiences he wants, and you want for him.

SITUATION: Your brother and sister-in-law happen to make a lot more money than you and love to shower your kids with wonderful gifts. But you can't reciprocate with their kids, and deep down you wish they wouldn't give your kids what you can't yourself.

ACTION: Stop feeling inferior. Stop thinking about this and just say something to them. You get to raise your children as you wish. Your siblings and in-laws should respect that, but first you have to respect yourself enough to speak for yourself.

SITUATION: Your teenager just came home with news that his school is arranging an educational trip to help build homes for needy families in a foreign country. You want to encourage him to help others and to learn more about the world, but the $1,800 needed to cover the airfare and travel costs is going to require that you tap your emergency savings fund.

ACTION: Okay, this is a tough one. You'd love to go on a great trip like this yourself, let alone provide your child with an amazing experience. But no one ever said good parenting was about always saying yes at any cost. I just can't abide sending your child on the trip if it puts your family's security at risk. This is one instance where I could get behind advancing your child money for the trip. That is, make a deal that he is to get a job to repay you for the cost, or maybe half the cost. That's up to you to work out; the point is that if he wants to go badly enough he will be motivated to contribute to the cost. You'll likely need to front him the money, but just work out a plan in which he agrees to repay you a certain amount each month. And you better hold him to it. For what it's worth, I bet he might even get more out of the trip knowing he financed some part of it himself.

SITUATION: You realize you've created a bit of a monster by constantly saying yes to your son: He is 15 and feels entitled to just about everything. You regret this, but you don't know how to start over and impart lessons in the value of money.

ACTION: Would it hurt to come clean? Sit your kid down and explain that you are worried that you have let him down by letting him think you are an endless ATM to be tapped. Tell him that you worry he has no clue about the value of money. So out of love, you are going to institute some new family financial habits.

Back-to-school is a great time to let kids loose with a fixed budget for clothes and supplies. Tell them how much they have to spend and then help them figure out how to make it cover their needs.

If you have been doling out allowance without any stipulations, that has got to change right now. You need your kids to fulfill certain tasks to earn that allowance. And people, good grades and good behavior are not part of the allowance deal. You do not pay children for behaving well. You expect that from them, not reward them for it.

SITUATION: You know you have a small window of opportunity to teach your teenager about credit and debt before she leaves for college, but you aren't sure whether to give her her own card or put her on your card as an authorized user.

ACTION: When your child is between the ages of 13 and 16, I would have her use a debit card on a bank account that you both have access to. Each month you deposit a set sum in the account and discuss with her what expenses she is to pay for with her debit card. A rule change that takes effect in July 2010 will require banks to specifically ask you if you want overdraft coverage on a debit card. You are to say no. Do you hear me? Banks have literally made billions letting customers charge more than they have left in their checking accounts; then they hit them with steep overdraft charges. The best move you can make for your child is to decline the overdraft coverage. If your child tries to buy something without sufficient funds, he or she will not be allowed to make the purchase. That's good! It is much better than running up big overdraft charges, and it's also a great way to learn basic cash management.

You both can keep track online, and I would sit down at least once a month to review how the spending is going. This is just a nice low-key way of giving her some responsibility, but with you still firmly at the controls. (One important step with debit cards: Check your account online every few days to make sure there are no suspect or unauthorized charges. If you report any fraudulent debit charges within a few days of the money being debited from your account, you will typically be fully reimbursed; if you let weeks or months go by, the debit card issuer is not legally required to cover the mistake.)

Once your daughter is 16, add her to one of your credit cards as an authorized user, but only if you have a FICO credit score of 720 or better. This serves two purposes. First, you want your daughter to get experience using the credit card. I would make it a ritual to have her sit with you when you pay the bill; read over the statement together. Beginning in February of 2010 credit card statements will have to show the cost and time it will take you to pay off the balance if you make only the minimum payment due each month. What a great eye-opening conversation starter that will be about the high cost of credit card debt! The other benefit is that as long as you continue to handle your credit card responsibly, your daughter will begin to piggyback on your FICO score. I would make it a priority to talk to her about how that FICO score is going to play a big role in her life in a few years. Explain how a good FICO score will make it easier for her to rent an apartment, get her own cellphone account, and open an account with the local utility without having to fork over a security deposit.

If your FICO score is not above 700, I wouldn't add your child to your card. Instead, have her apply for a secured credit card—you can help her make the required deposit. A secured card works just like a credit card in terms of where you can use it. The only difference is that a deposit is required to open the account and your child's credit limit will be limited to the amount on deposit. The card is "secured" by that deposit. Just make sure the secured card reports her bill payment history to at least one credit bureau so she can start building a solid credit history of her own. You can call the credit card company's customer service and ask them if they report.

Beginning in 2010, credit card issuers will no longer be able to give accounts to a person under the age of 21 unless he or she has verifiable income that can cover the payments, or an adult cosigns for the card. This is great news. The sad fact is that too many kids are graduating from college with thousands of dollars in high-interest-rate credit card debt because the card issuers were handing out cards at freshman orientation like ice cream sandwiches on a hot beach.

Once your child heads to college you can talk about cosigning for a credit card, but you must set clear parameters about how this will work. You set the credit limit, and only you can request it be raised. Both of you have access to the account online. Your child is to pay the bill each month; in fact, it is to be automatically paid from a checking account. But you are to set up an email alert (as a cosigner you have access to the account) if the bill is unpaid.

SITUATION: You told your child you would send her to a private college, but you now realize you need to focus on other goals, such as building an emergency savings account and putting money away for retirement.

ACTION: The more honest you are today, the happier you and your child will be in the future. I know it is hard to contemplate changing your strategy, but doing what is right is often not easy. Making this hard choice could be what determines your future security. I want all parents to seriously rethink what they can afford to spend on college, be it through loans or out-of-pocket savings. The best school for your child is one that provides a solid education and doesn't put the family $150,000 to $200,000 in debt. I have no patience for anyone who tells me "cost is not the issue— a quality education is more important." *People, cost is a huge issue.* You can't afford to take on debt that keeps you from being able to pay your bills or to save for your retirement. Nor does it make sense to let your child pile up $100,000 in private student loans. Student loan debt, in most cases, is not forgiven in bankruptcy. It is the Velcro of debt; you cannot shake loose from it. Student loan debt will make it that much harder for your children to build their own financial security after they graduate. When you have a lot of student loan debt, it makes it harder to qualify for a mortgage or a car loan. And I cannot tell you how many smart, well-intentioned young adults tell me they had no idea how much their monthly payments would be and they cannot afford to pay them at all.

Keep an open mind: Look for affordable schools, starting, of course, with your in-state college system. A quality education is not dependent on price. You can find a great fit for your child and your finances if you make it a priority. Go to Kiplinger .com and under "Your Money" click on "Best College Values."

SITUATION: Your son got into his first choice for college. He is thrilled. You are proud. But his backup school is offering a financial aid package that will cost you $18,000 less a year, and that would be a big help in allowing you to save more for retirement rather than take on debt to cover the college costs. But you can't imagine asking your child to settle for anything less than his first choice.

ACTION: The goal is a college education that is affordable. Don't forget the affordable part. At the risk of repeating myself, I will remind you that there are no scholarships or loans for retirement; you are on your own. If one college would leave you in much better financial shape than another college, walk through the math with your son. He'll get it. The more you can save now, the less likely you will need his help when he is just starting out and has his own young family to support.

But I also want you to check with his first-choice school; let them know the package you are being offered at the backup. There is no harm in seeing if his aid package can be increased. If not, school number two it is.

SITUATION: Your daughter, a junior in college, just came clean that she has $5,000 in credit card debt. You aren't sure if you should bail her out, especially since it will mean dipping into your emergency savings.

ACTION: This is all too common. And to be honest, it's not entirely your kid's fault. You may have dropped the ball on instilling credit card basics before she went off to school; also, as I mentioned earlier, not long ago the card companies were relentless in signing up clueless kids to cards and letting them charge away. So you need to size up the situation. The last thing we want is for that $5,000 to continue to rack up more interest charges; nor do we want it to spiral so far out of control that it absolutely decimates her FICO score. So help may be appropriate, but only if you can afford it, and only if you attach some strings.

The absolute worst thing you can do is write the check and wipe out the debt without any lessons learned. I am telling you that anyone, at any age, who is let off the hook without being held accountable is apt to repeat the behavior again. That's not the goal.

So here's your plan: If you can cover the payment and still have eight months of living expenses left in your emergency fund, you have no credit card debt, and your retirement savings are in great shape, I will approve your paying the bill. But only if you and your daughter have a written agreement that she is to pay you back every month starting right now. No interest. But each month she is to pay you X dollars. That's her lesson in responsibility. However, if paying the bill in full would take your emergency fund below eight months' worth of coverage, or would put a dent in your other financial goals, then I need you to face facts: You can't afford to help her financially. You can help her plot out a repayment plan.

Once that is squared away, sit down and talk through those credit card basics you should have covered a few years ago. Do not reprimand. You can't blame a child for not knowing something no one ever bothered to explain. You could do worse than having her read the chapter in this book about credit!

SITUATION: Your college senior announced she wants to take a year off before entering the "real world"—especially since jobs are so scarce—and trek through Europe. As much as you see the value in this great life experience, paying for it isn't exactly in your budget.

ACTION: Give her your blessings, but do not give her a penny. Your budget is already stretched thin, and you are actually contemplating helping to pay for this adventure? Come on, that's crazy. This isn't about denying her, it's about taking care of your important financial goals (such as making sure you're not a future financial burden on her in your retirement). If she wants to have this adventure badly enough, she will figure out how to pay for it. She's a college grad; this is definitely within her capabilities. She's your daughter, but she's no longer a kid. Okay?

Maybe she has to move home for six months and get a job to save up enough to finance whatever shortfall exists. Make it clear you are 100% behind this adventure, that you are so excited for her, but you also need her to understand you have competing financial needs: retirement, paying off the mortgage, maybe a sibling still in college. So she needs to step up and finance this adventure on her own.

SITUATION: Your son is graduating from college and wants to move back home to save money. You're not sure if that's a good thing or a step back from his becoming a fully independent adult.

ACTION: Discuss your child's goals for moving back in. Is it some sort of free-formed notion that moving back is a cheap alternative to reality that comes with built-in laundry, room service, and housekeeping? Those are not acceptable terms for you. Here's what I suggest: Write up a one-page agreement that covers his financial obligation and codes of conduct.

First the finances: If he has a job, you must charge rent. I don't care if it is $50 a week, it has to be something. Whatever you charge it must include his share of the utilities and food. This is especially important if your kid lived on campus all four years and has no clue what it costs to cover basic necessities. If that makes you queasy, stick the money in a savings account, and when your child finally moves out, give him all the rent back to help him with his new place.

If your child is looking for work, you need to be supportive, but you do not need to be his personal Ritz-Carlton. I would go back to chores. Only this time it can be picking up the groceries, doing the laundry, maybe even running your errands for you. Sure you want your kid to focus on job hunting, but that's not a 12-hour-a-day job. He can work for you an hour or two a day.

I also want you to set a move-out date. Not because you don't love him, but for exactly the reason that you love him so much. Let's face it, your place is cushy compared to the rental that will be in his price range. That reduces his motivation to move out. So you need to apply a firm but loving nudge.

SITUATION: Your 23-year-old daughter wants you to cosign for a new car loan.

ACTION: Denied. Why does your child need a *new* car? There are plenty of used cars, including certified pre-owned cars with just a year or two of wear and tear that have great warranties and cost a lot less. And you need to ask yourself why she needs you to cosign. Is it for more than she can honestly handle on her salary? Is it because her FICO credit score is so bad the lender insists on you coming in as a safety net? And let's review the basics of cosigning: You become legally responsible for the loan in the event your daughter falls behind. Don't think you can let her just learn a lesson if the car is repossessed. It's *your* FICO score that is going to take a hit, not just hers.

SITUATION: Your son and daughter-in-law are in mortgage trouble. You are retired and are considering using some of your savings to help them through this rough patch.

ACTION: If you can afford to help, then of course help. But that's a serious issue you need to carefully ponder. If helping them out today in any way puts your own retirement security at risk, then you simply cannot afford to help. That's not being selfish, it's actually looking out for your kids. You need to think through how this could play out. You help the kids out now, but that means your retirement account runs dry in 15 years instead of lasting the 25 or 30 years you were counting on. And let's say you have the good fortune of living a very long life. Only problem is, you need to turn to your kids for help because you no longer have any money left.

You have the valuable assets in this situation. You probably own your own home outright and you have a nice retirement fund. Do not put those at risk. If your kids are in a house they can't afford, it may be best for them to let go. If they live nearby, you can offer to have them move in while they regroup. Or if they are determined to stay in the house, how about you offer to take a more active role helping with the grandkids on the weekends so they can take on part-time work—or extra projects at their job—to bring in the income they need.

10

The Right Way

You hold in your hands all the financial rules, principles, and strategies you need to put you on a path to building lasting financial security. You have your Action Plan for the road ahead.

I realize there is a lot to digest here. For many of you there will be much to change. Please give yourself the time and patience to make the necessary renovations. And understand that this isn't a weekend project. It is a lifelong commitment to taking care of yourself and your loved ones. That doesn't mean you must spend every free moment strategizing about money issues. That is just the opposite of why I devised this Action Plan. My goal is that once you take control of your financial life—by taking action—you won't spend so much of your life feeling stressed about money. I am asking you to pay attention to your money now in order to free up your life so you can . . . well, *live* your life. That's what financial freedom has always meant to me—and what every book I've written aims to do: to give you time to enjoy your life without financial fear defining who you are and what you can achieve.

That's been quite a challenge since the financial crisis struck in 2008. The shock and severity of the meltdown has been crushing. Pondering your family's financial security is nerve-racking enough, but there's also the not-so-small issue of our nation's economic health to keep you on edge too.

I can guarantee you one thing: Worry won't get you where you want to go. Action is the only way out from under the stress. What I have laid out for you in this book are your steppingstones; each action moves you toward the ultimate goal: peace of mind and security. The financial crisis and its aftershocks are holding you hostage right now; the Action Plan is your path to freedom.

My focus is on you, but I also know that as each of us repairs what is not working in our personal lives it will help us move forward collectively. The crisis has taught us that our actions not only affect our individual lives, they have an impact on the collective whole, on systems, and on the very fate and health of our nation. The calls for integrity and responsibility should be heard by every one of us, no matter who you are, no matter what your station. This is a time of renewal, of recommitment. Obviously it would have been preferable if we made these seismic changes from a position of strength and not in reaction to crisis. But in a way, the enormity of the turmoil will ultimately pay dividends for all of us; it was so bad, it was—*is*—so destabilizing, that we can't shrug it off. It is a life changer. For my money, those changes will all be for good.

Adjusting to the New Rules for New Times means that it's not likely you will ever feel this scared and insecure again. Don't misunderstand; bad times will recur. They are as inevitable as the good times. But the opportunity before you right now is to rebuild your financial life so that, should the storm winds pick up again, you will not be blown away.

For all the specific rules and regulations, principles and practices I am asking you to learn and follow, I want you to realize they all emanate from a single simple law:

Do what is right, not what is easy.

When you find yourself with a choice to make— vacation versus Roth IRA contribution; school trip versus funding the 529 account; retiring early versus staying on the job a few more years— consciously ask yourself this: Which is the one that will help me and my family build long-term security? Ask yourself if you have the determination and the courage to make the right choice.

And when you feel overwhelmed or frustrated, stop what you are doing and tell yourself, literally tell yourself: *I am doing what is right, not what is easy.* Find strength in that singular commitment. It takes courage and resolve to remake what is not right. Give yourself credit every day. And know that every step along the way, every right action you take, moves you closer to a life you are free to live to the fullest. You deserve that now more than ever.